THE POWER
&THE GLORY

Reach Sport

THE POWER & THE GLORY

Mick Clegg

WITH STEVE BARTRAM

This book is dedicated to our heavenly father and his son, Jesus Christ, our saviour and high priest, who have been there for me whenever I appealed to them. Even through periods when I sinned and neglected them, they forgave me, healed me and helped me throughout my life.

Reach Sport

www.reachsport.com

Published in Great Britain and Ireland in 2022 by
Reach Sport, a Reach PLC business,
5 St Paul's Square, Liverpool, L3 9SJ.

www.reachsport.com
@Reach_Sport

Reach Sport is a part of Reach PLC.
One Canada Square, Canary Wharf, London, E15 5AP.

Hardback ISBN: 9781914197376
eBook ISBN: 9781914197383

Photographic acknowledgements:
Mick Clegg personal collection, Reach PLC.
Every effort has been made to trace the copyright.
Any oversight will be rectified in future editions.

Edited and produced by Simon Monk.
Design: Rick Cooke. Additional production: Harri Aston.

Printed and bound by CPI Group (UK) Ltd,
Croydon, CR0 4YY.

Contents

Foreword by Cristiano Ronaldo

When I first joined Manchester United in 2003, I wanted to become the best player I could possibly be.

At that time, I was only 18 years old, so I knew that I had a long journey ahead of me. I had to get to know my new team-mates, learn a new language and settle into a new life. There was a lot for me to do and a lot of pressure on me, being a young signing for United, but my attitude has always been to cope with the pressure by working hard.

At a club the size of United, all the tools were there for you to improve if you were prepared to put in the effort. One of the best ways to improve yourself, I soon found, was by working with Mick, or 'Cleggy' as everybody called him.

In my early days at the club, we had some great conversations where I explained what I wanted to achieve and what I wanted to do better, and he explained to me exactly how I could do it through work in the gym at Carrington. So we listened to each other and worked hard together. I always wanted to do extra work in the gym and Mick was always there for me, even though he was very busy helping so many other players. The work we did was very specific, very clever and along with the work I was doing on other aspects of my game, it helped me to improve massively.

As my career developed, one or two trophies became many more and I consider myself very fortunate to have won so many honours, both in a team and as an individual. A big part of my success has been how well I have taken care of my body, because if you are in the wrong condition then you can't play your best football. I put in a lot of work to keep in the best condition I can be in, and a lot of my success in that area stems from what I learnt with Mick.

I always want to learn and improve and I think Mick feels the same way about his own life. He was an incredible coach, a massive help to me and a great character.

Cristiano Ronaldo, January 2022

Acknowledgements

My first one-on-one encounter with Mick was an eye-opener.

It was late 2011. I'd driven to Portland Mill in Ashton to interview him about Darren Fletcher's recent return to fitness. I heaved my 90kgs up the three flights of stairs and, on Mick's invitation, crammed into his tiny office to wait while he finished brewing up.

While I waited, I scoured his bookshelf, which I've always regarded as a window of insight into the psyche of the books' owners. The subject material was arresting. Quantum physics and numerology were flanked by vampirism and the Bible.

Eyebrow cocked, interest piqued.

After Mick returned, it didn't take long to get the material I needed on Fletch. Thereafter, amidst two hours' overmatter on various topics, it became clear to me what the real story was. This man was a raconteur, pure and simple.

"You should write a book," I said.

"A few people have said that," he responded. "Come back next week, same time."

Over the next decade, we took turns to lament that exchange. Momentum came and went as life got in the way. Divorce (mine), health concerns (his) and parenting (ours) all contributed to the staccato. Mick was disenchanted enough to suggest scrapping the whole idea on more than one occasion, while I would frequently ask myself his catchphrase, 'What the fuck are you doing here?' as surprises were routinely sprung upon me. A particular favourite came in early on, when he suggested going out for a meal with his family to get to know everyone, only to learn mid-starter that I was chairing a brainstorming meeting for the Clegg brand.

That, I guess, is part of the magic of the man. Everything is a test to be passed and I flunked a fair few during the process of this book. I owe a debt of thanks to a broad range of people for their help and support in getting here – not least my wife Kerry (who must have contemplated, at least briefly, that I was having a particularly unlikely affair) and my kids, Emily and Charlie, whose interest in the project helped keep me going through the home straight.

The incomparable Michael Calvin, one of the best writers in the business, very kindly took time out of his schedule to give me invaluable pointers on how to approach co-writing an autobiography, Stu Garneys worked wonders with his camera, as did Paul Dove, Rick Cooke, Simon Monk at Reach Sport.

For me, a final shout-out goes to all of Mick's family and colleagues – past and present – who were kind enough to spare their valuable time and pay tribute to him. Mick has, by his own admission, been somewhat abrasive down the years, so it was both a huge relief and an enormous validation of the project to hear so many glowing tributes. Having interviewed a lot of footballers in my time, I can't recall anyone receiving such unanimously positive praise.

The main man, meanwhile, would also like to thank his kids for being his ultimate crash test dummies. He loves them, their partners and children dearly. Beyond that, he is indebted to every single athlete who has ever entrusted their wellbeing to him, since they have each provided him with invaluable and innumerable lessons. On an operational side, Gary Sloane, Mark Hagan, Tom Traynor, Lisa Hovelsen, David Hobson, Adam Hobson and Lee Sidebottom have helped him at every turn, Julie Demeza and Lee Clark have provided endless hospitality and breakfasts while Wayne and Diane Topping have given priceless spiritual and emotional guidance throughout this deeply reflective process.

Furthermore, he was shocked to his core by the death of Rocky 2, but now has another Alsatian in his life, named 'T'. This has allowed him to form special new friendships with Alex and a crackpot Staffy named Digger, and he cherishes the time they all spend together.

As you would imagine when a book takes a decade to write, it hasn't been a smooth process from start to finish. At the end of that first meeting at Portland Mill, I dubbed Mick 'the wise man', a moniker he still laughs off.

Exactly a decade to the day after that encounter, I was driving to his lab, just before 6am on a dank November morning, aquaplaning along the M60 in fittingly biblical rain when it occurred to me that this was the first-world equivalent of venturing into the Himalayas to visit a mystic. It's an arduous, ambitious, breathtakingly stupid idea, with the potential to be either life-ending or life-changing.

I'm 10 years into knowing him and I can happily say that it has been emphatically the latter. You don't meet many Mick Cleggs in life and I'm so proud to call him a friend. This book has been an undulating, oscillating trip from soul-destroying to soul-soaring, and easily the biggest challenge of my professional career so far, but it has been one of the very greatest honours of my life to hear and share his story.

Mick and I agreed very early on that, even though he had a ringside seat for so much salacious material down the years, this book wouldn't be about sensationalism. Some tales will forever remain secrets of the Carrington gym. Instead, we wanted to tell his story, put his message out there and throw in a few anecdotes along the way for entertainment and insight.

As a person and a coach, he's always aimed to improve himself and help others improve themselves. If one individual reads this book and becomes a better coach, parent or athlete as a result of Mick's learnings and teachings, then they can pay forward his wisdom and help others to help others. That, we agreed, would be truly powerful work.

Steve Bartram, Manchester, January 2022

Preface: Why are you here?

What the fuck are you doing here?

It's a brilliant question, isn't it? If you're being asked that question in any setting, it demands your focus. It demands your consideration.

It demands an answer.

"What the fuck are you doing here?"

That has always been the first question I've asked anybody I'm about to coach, whether it was at my family gym, the gym at Manchester United's Carrington training ground or the performance lab I now run in Ashton.

It might sound aggressive – especially barked out in my dulcet northern tones – and it certainly does bring a momentarily startled look to a lot of faces, but I can assure you that it's the most important question any athlete can be asked because it forces them to examine their own motives.

Why am I here?

What do I want to achieve?

Once they've got their answer straight in their own minds, they can share that motivation with me and I, as their coach, know exactly what we're aiming for. Then we can get to work.

As a rule, I've tended to keep a fairly low profile during the course of my career. I'm a coach. Now that my kids are all grown up, that's pretty much the limit of what I do. So, when my name crops up in any kind of public arena, you can count on it being about my coaching. Specifically, it's usually about my time at Manchester United. More often than not, you can guarantee it will be in relation to Cristiano Ronaldo. He's one of the most famous footballers – and one of the greatest athletic specimens – in the history of sport, so to have played any part in his story at all is a huge personal and professional thrill. He's also very useful when it comes to illustrating my original point.

The first time I ever came into contact with Cristiano, I asked him what he was doing in the Carrington gym.

As is often the case with players for whom English is a second language, especially young lads, he developed a quizzical look on his face while he decoded what this strange little man was saying to him. He was very new to the country and his English wasn't yet the best, so it took another prompt:

"Why have you walked through this door?"

This time he understood.

"I want to be the best. You will help me."

As a coach, that's the answer you dream about. A coach is there to facilitate improvement, but that can only reach as far as the limit of the athlete's ambition. When you come into contact with an athlete whose ambition is boundless, then you have manna from heaven.

I've been very, very fortunate to have crossed paths with a lot of unbelievable athletes during my life. At every intersection, I've tried to do my very best by them all, whether they were an established world star at the peak of their profession, an up-and-coming talent, a youngster looking to better themselves in amateur sport or my own kids.

Every working relationship I've built in over 40 years of coaching has begun with that simple question: what are you doing here? You're probably asking yourself the same question now. *Why am I holding this book?*

Your reasons are your own. Chances are, you're interested to hear about life inside Carrington, working with some of the best footballers ever to play the game under arguably the greatest manager ever to occupy a dugout. It might be about fitness regimes or running a gym. It could be about coaching kids – even your own.

I've been encouraged to write a book by a number of people down the years. I never took much notice, but one man kept on at me, saying that he'd write it with me. It's taken Steve and I a long time to get here, during which time I've had a huge range of new experiences which have added fresh thoughts and observations, but I think it's a story worth sharing. I'm a little old man now, but there are people out there who can learn from what I've done.

When I look back on my experiences and ask myself, in hindsight, what I was doing there, I can only conclude one thing: I was trying my best to help people better themselves. I've had decades of experiences: a lot of good, a lot of bad. I've built unbreakable relationships and seen others crumble. I've known the full gamut of parenting. I've seen what it takes to guide an elite athlete and help them maximise their talent. I've seen how incredible gifts can be squandered. I've seen a lot and I want to share it.

I hope you find something in these pages which informs, entertains or inspires you.

Mick Clegg, Ashton-under-Lyne, January 2022

CHAPTER 1

Girls And Guitars

"Thankfully, I was able to make inner peace with being a short-arse."

I'm just a coach. That's what I always tell people around me.

It must do their heads in at times, because whenever they ask me to do anything that falls outside the duties of a coach, that's my riposte. They probably have a lot of different names for me but as far as I'm concerned I'm just a coach. That's all I've ever been any good at. That's me.

Specifically, I'm a power development coach, and I think that has been my purpose, if you like, from the start of my life. Believe it or not, I was born overlooking a power station, so the scene was set for me from day one.

My dad was a fireman at the local power station in Heyrod, Stalybridge, near Manchester, and his job was a simple act which kept huge processes moving: he'd put the coal on the chain grate bed that goes into the fire, which heats up the water, that turns into steam, that turns the turbine, that rotates the generator, which then produces electricity. From my very beginnings, I was involved in power, with electricity being an awesome power to start off. Fail to give electricity its due respect and you can be dead in a split second.

We then went to New Romney in Kent when my dad got a transfer to a nuclear power station. As I got older, I began to pick up more understanding of what he did. We kept moving around, then we came back up north, so he could go back to work at Heyrod power station again, and he told me that I had to get a job. Although both my parents struggled with alcoholism, I listened to what they said. My dad wanted me to work with him, so I became an electrical engineer at Heyrod. I studied it at college too, so my studying was all about how to produce power.

Everywhere I turned, power fascinated me. When I was a kid, I loved comic books like the *Fantastic Four*, *The Incredible Hulk* and *Spider-Man*. Ever since those formative years, I've always believed that we're all capable of being superhuman, and a very important part of the philosophy I've developed in my own life is the search for that magic ingredient to transform an ordinary person into a superhuman. For the Hulk it was gamma rays, for Spider-Man it was a radioactive spider-bite, but I've always believed there's something in the brain of everyday, normal people that can provoke superhuman powers.

Some people are able to tap into these abilities, and not just in a sporting sense. There are geniuses in all sorts of fields – mathematics, science, music or arts; there are autistic people who can read thousands of words in a minute – so, as I've gone through life, what has always fascinated me is whether there's a way of giving us control over these abilities. I believe there is, and it's all about finding people who have these attributes and can share their experiences to show how their abilities can be harnessed. Of course, I wasn't thinking about that in such a way when I was a kid. As a teenage boy,

I mainly thought about girls. After we'd come back up north and I was attending Hartshead High School, my thoughts tended to focus on one particular girl: Sue Bardsley. She was the prettiest girl in our school and, even though I was a little short-arse who had come up from down south, I was probably better at talking to people than other lads my age. I'd already become accustomed to making new friendships in every new place my dad's work had taken us – I went to nine different schools during my childhood – and I was basically forced to gain friends or be lonely, and loneliness is a cruelty I could not live with.

So, I had experience of talking to girls. That's not to say I was a gifted sweet-talker who could leave them all swooning; I could just string a few words together when everyone else was grunting monosyllabically at them. Anyway, I wasn't going to complain.

They were different times back then. Nowadays when I have teenage kids coming into my gym, they're courting in an altogether different way to how it used to be done. I can't imagine what it would have been like to grow up in the modern age, with such a different stance on relationships and marriage, with the ability to chat to people in different hemispheres through a video call on a phone I could put in my pocket, but I do know that things were much simpler for me back then.

When I was 15, I fancied the prettiest girl in our school. When I was 16, I asked her out. We got engaged at 17 and by the time I was 18, I'd married her and bought a house.

I'm sure you can guess what the next step was for me at 19. In July 1977, exactly nine months and a day after we married, Sue and I had our first child: Michael Jamie Clegg.

We were thrilled and I was shocked by the amount of responsibility I had already built into my life. I was happy. I had everything I could want. Long before my 20th birthday, I was a homeowner, college student, breadwinner, husband and father.

I still had ambitions for the future, however, and they centred on the guitar.

Having started playing at 16, I had begun to make some progress and I was in and out of a few bands. My vision was clear: the music industry was to be my future vocation. In the meantime, I needed my job in the power station to finance everything that I was to do going forward.

When you learn the guitar, a very important aspect is learning to multi-task; one hand fingering the strings, the other hand plucking the strings, while reading music, while tapping your foot to keep the beat, and I used to sing as well. Now, to be completely clear, I sang and played very badly. Anybody who heard me would confirm as much and I never, ever had a chance of pursuing music as a career. But it allowed me to multi-task from an early age.

I eventually got into a band called Stroller, playing bass guitar, and we were working the Yorkshire circuit. We decided to have some flyers made to whip up interest, so we got a photographer down to capture us in all our glory. This proved to be a pivotal moment in my life because, when I saw the pictures from the shoot, one thing immediately struck me.

My arms. They were skinnier than the strings on my guitar.

I was mortified. And so, for literally no other reason than good, old-fashioned vanity, I started going to the local gym, which was called Shapes, in Ashton-under-Lyne.

Within six months, I was coaching other people inside the gym; not because I was suddenly a strapping Adonis rippling with big muscles, but because I really understood the mechanics of what I was doing. I couldn't tell you exactly why, but I just got it. Lift *this* in *this* particular way, and it achieves *this* result. It seemed simple to me. People around the gym noticed that I knew what I was doing and then, for reasons only they know, they would ask me questions. I was happy enough to help and that led into me coaching people.

The resident coach and owner of Shapes, who went by the suitably meaty name of Big Stanny and had biceps literally bigger than my head, came over one day and enquired: "I'm the coach in here, how come you're coaching everybody?" Immediately I was on the defensive and protested that I was just answering people's questions. He calmed me down and said: "Don't worry about it. People like your personality, they listen to what you're saying and what you're saying tallies with what I've always thought." He asked me to take on a part-time coaching role at Shapes and, alongside my position at the power station, I ended up coaching there for the next two years until it closed down. I don't think it closed down because of me, for the record, and I suppose the good news for the music industry is that having even more demands on my time sounded a death knell for my short career as a noodle-armed guitarist.

* * *

In the early 1980s, there was a huge interest in bodybuilding, particularly in Arnold Schwarzenegger, Franco Columbu and that type of figure, and I was besotted with the movement.

I bought magazines and devoured them. I went to watch bodybuilding events. Throughout my early 20s, I regarded it as the ultimate sport. I looked at these huge, rippling guys and just saw a triumph of the physical form. I took a massive interest in nutrition as well because, of course, without proper nutrition then all the training was just a waste of time. It wasn't until a few years later that I realised a lot of people on those stages owed their physiques to other factors, rather than good nutrition.

Though Shapes was sadly no more, my coaching continued with my own kids. By the time Michael was six, he had two major developments in his life: his younger brother, Mark, and an absolute obsession with *Monkey*, the old kung-fu television show. So, when I was walking with Michael and pushing Mark along in his pushchair one evening in Ashton and we happened upon a taekwondo gym at the back of Ashton Old Baths, Michael inevitably wanted to get involved. Since I had enjoyed advising people in the gym and had already seen that I could help them improve physically, I'd decided that I wanted Michael to get involved with weights from an early age. I wanted to help him be strong.

So, I spoke to the guy running the place, Alan Horton, who was a taekwondo master despite only having one eye, and I asked him if I could use part of his gym to do some weights with Michael as well as my own training. Nothing major, just some basic weighted moves like squats and bicep curls, using tiny dumbbells.

Alan had no problem with that and, within a few weeks, he saw the weights work I was doing with Michael and asked me to train him too. Just as it had at Shapes, my coaching snowballed. Within a short time I was training Alan's wife, his kids, his friends and others were joining in too, so the clientele just kept growing.

Alan mentioned to me after a few months that he was arranging a sponsored walk to raise money for new equipment in the gym. He asked me to join in and, while I wasn't averse to the idea, because of my bodybuilding obsession I suggested to him as an alternative that we could run a Strongest Man in Tameside event, with the proceeds going towards funding the gym equipment. Through my time at Shapes, I knew people at various fitness clubs in the area, so I went around raising awareness of the event and encouraging people to partake. We were inundated with entries.

Even though it was mainly big guys who turned up, since it was also a taekwondo gym we didn't just make the categories weights-based. We did deadlifts, clean-and-jerks and some of the usual weightlifting staples, but we also did sit-ups and press-ups within the competition, so it wasn't just about lifting massive amounts of weight. Michael, who had been training really hard at this stage, won the sit-ups section of the competition even though he was only seven or eight at that stage – it sounds like a fix but I can promise you it wasn't. He was incredible.

The event was such a success that Alan suggested that we started opening the gym an hour earlier than usual so that I could provide weight training before the taekwondo sessions.

The more I coached, the more I learnt. Listening, I soon realised, is paramount in coaching. When someone comes to you, you have to listen to them and find out their story, find out what they're looking for. You recognise the information that's necessary to tap into their hidden mind, and that hidden mind reveals everything. Stories that I've been told by doctors, nurses, ex-Marines, anybody I've worked with, they all shed light on the emotional reason that they're in the gym. If you listen to them, listen to their stories, then you begin to understand why each individual is there. It didn't take me long to realise that coaching isn't about just bicep curls, tendons, ligaments, insertions into the bone and the sheer mechanics of the body; it's the understanding of the deep psychology of the person.

As this realisation began to fully dawn on me, I spent six months working with a hypnotist to understand more about the mind, which was an invaluable experience. For starters, he showed me that I had my perception of myself all wrong. He said that how I saw myself and my feelings were both way off the mark; they were altered images of my true self. I wanted this guy to plant a seed in my mind, something that would help me work towards growing bigger and stronger. I had this idea that if you could concentrate your mind so deeply into what you wanted to achieve, you could then make that happen.

Basically, this guy said: "You're five foot six, but you want to be six foot six. You're trying to change your size. You can't do that no matter how much concentrating you do. Meditate all you want, have as much hypnosis as you want, I can't make you grow another foot in height."

As he uncovered more and more about my mentality, it just fuelled my interest in the workings of the mind. He made me understand that what we need to focus on are the things that are possible, because if you go along with the things that are possible then you can build them up. If you're trying to make something that's impossible happen, you'll just wear yourself out and break down. That's what a lot of people do: hope that something is going to happen and go down that pathway, but at the end of the path is a big ditch into which they slip and get trapped. You convince yourself that something can happen, you realise that it can't and then you don't know how to get out of that ditch. This is how a lot of people turn to alcohol and drugs. Thankfully, I was able to make inner peace with being a short-arse.

Within a short time, I had an all-consuming distraction because Alan Horton fell ill and asked me to take over the running of the taekwondo gym while he was in hospital. He never really came back fully and, in his absence, the martial arts clientele began to dwindle because one of the coaches (who taught kickboxing with a little too much gusto) kept beating them up. While I was in charge, I naturally had much more interest in the gym side of the operation than the taekwondo side, so I just carried on building my own business in there from that point. In the late summer of 1984, that included relocating to Portland Mill nearby. Ashton Old Baths had become a mess and the building had to be renovated, so I moved the premises to what would soon become Olympic Sports Gym.

In that first week in the new premises, among a host of new clients were three wise men who would go on to feature regularly in my life over the coming years: Gary Boulton, who is still now competing in World Powerlifting events, even though he's in his 50s; John Sweeney, who was a fireman who trained in kickboxing and became my training partner over the following decades; then Frank Morris, who became something of a business mentor over the years. Frank had no particular career when I met him, but he decided to become a welder and he learnt that you needed to clean metal before welding it. From that discovery, he went on to make fortunes with a metal-cleaning business. I met Gary, John and Frank in the same week and they all remain a part of my life almost 40 years on. The three of them aren't just clients, they became important parts of my learning curve and were great listeners to me because, like anybody, I also needed someone to speak to at various points down the years.

They were among the founders of a client base which grew steadily, but it was my family who were central to what soon began to unfold.

CHAPTER 2

Young Prospects

"The kids at the school wanted to get away from the issues affecting Moss Side in the 1990s – stabbings, muggings and gun crime."

As things grew and grew, my kids became utterly crucial to me not just as a parent, but as a coach.

Just under three years after Michael was born, Mark came along. Again, just under three years later, like clockwork, Steven was born. Slightly further down the line, Mandy and Shaun completed the family line-up. I was still an electrical engineer for Norweb by day and I'd run Olympic Sports Gym in the evening, all the while training the kids and allowing them to grow up in and around an athletic environment. They had a unique upbringing in that sense. Shaun was literally 13 months old when he would be picking up the one-kilo weightlifting plate with both hands and slowly tottering around the gym with his nappy on.

As the eldest, Michael led the way in what was happening. By the time he was a teenager, he would come to the gym straight from his school – Stamford High School in Ashton – open up and let people in while I was still at work. Michael had a nice way about him and was very popular, not only with everyone around the gym, but also at school. A lot of his mates were soon piling into our gym and they were all training together. Michael was extremely dedicated to his training, so his mates followed that example. They were kids, but there wasn't a lot of messing around; they were there to work hard.

Suddenly, the school teams started doing well as a result of this. They excelled at football and basketball in particular. Their improvement was so noticeable that Mike Madden, the school's PE teacher, came down to see what was making such a difference to all his pupils. I walked him through everything I was doing with them. He was so taken with what he saw that I was offered a job teaching his pupils about fitness. He would bring classes to the gym and I'd speak about training, diets and good lifestyle habits.

I very much specialised in working with kids at this time and I decided to introduce Olympic weightlifting to their training. I received a grant from Tameside Council, bought a bar and weights from the Russian Weightlifting Federation and was able to get a reporter from the local paper to tell people what we were doing.

'Strengthening our Local Children' was the headline.

Things started taking off. We got a junior weightlifting team off the ground, competing locally and doing quite well. My second eldest, Mark, became very prominent in this. He was around 14 at the time, and up until a couple of years prior had been almost a total non-athlete. He'd dabbled in taekwondo and karate from the age of 12, but suddenly he exploded into the local basketball scene. He was brilliant. Crucially, he started weightlifting to help with his basketball training and, just as Michael's friends had followed him, Mark's friends suddenly wanted to train with him and be around him all the time.

Our house and garden became the local youth club, to the extent that we put a basketball court in the back garden. Sue absolutely loved that. At a time when the news regularly mentioned gangs and gun violence among youths, she really encouraged the kids to have their friends piling in because she knew they were safe. The number of boys and girls coming and going from our house and the gym was amazing. I was spending most of my time working with kids aged 12 to 16 throughout this period, and giving talks to classes from Stamford evolved into working with other schools, then colleges and I began to become fairly well known around Ashton for what I was doing.

Through it all, I was relentless in my attempts to keep developing myself and my craft. I noticed that a lot of weightlifting coaches were using techniques that, although good for adults, were potentially damaging for the kids because their bodies hadn't developed enough to handle the demands being placed upon them. I took on my own approach that was modified for juniors. The standard model was that you get your weights bar on the floor and 'clean' it, or pull it up to your chest.

For weightlifters in proper competitions, they do this with a heavy weight and then drop right underneath it, to the point that their backsides are practically on the floor. That's fine for trained adults, but for a kid to drop under weights like that was ridiculous. They'd either drop under the bar and couldn't stand up, or they'd fall over or spill the bar.

So, I made sure my lads were lifting weights that they could catch and hold, but only bending their legs slightly instead of going into a full squat like everybody else. Then, once they'd got the weight under control, they could stand up and do the second part, the 'jerk', which is lifting the bar above your head. My way – technically speaking, a 'power clean' into the 'jerk' – was much more mechanically efficient. Other coaches complained that we were doing it differently, so we checked through the rules and it never stated anywhere that the weightlifter had to drop below the bar, much less into a full squat, so their complaints were baseless.

The established method of lifting was designed for adults, not kids, and it posed all kinds of issues for knees, hips and backs, so it needed to evolve in the junior area or risk doing damage.

The results were spectacular. Not only did we dramatically increase the boys' control of the weights and lower their risk of injury (our injury record was miles better than that of anybody else on the circuit), we ended up going around the country winning everything. I became very unpopular with other coaches on the circuit as a result, but the changes I'd made to training within the field opened doors for me, and I ended up taking on lots of higher qualifications within weightlifting. Of all the sports I've coached, that's the area in which I'm officially the most qualified.

I learned about plyometrics at this time and I saw the potential partnership it would play with weightlifting to create superior athletes. Basically, it entails using maximum strength in short bursts of time. I introduced this type of training and the results were almost instant. The lads that I was training for football, basketball and weightlifting benefited greatly from plyometrics. They all became so much more powerful and that came to the fore at one school sports day across

Tameside. Stamford won so many events that other coaches really started to take notice of what we were doing.

* * *

My work in schools continued to expand all the time. I opened a gym in Ducie High School, Moss Side, and started working with the pupils. There was a real appetite among the kids to get out of the area whenever they could because they wanted to get away from the issues affecting Moss Side in the early-to-mid-1990s, which were stabbings, muggings and gun crime. I put this to the school and they agreed that every Friday night I could use the school bus, take a load of their kids over to Olympic in Ashton, train them and then drop them back home again afterwards. Those pupils weren't content to just be out of Moss Side for a night each week, either; they put in the graft and that group won the British Weightlifting Championships at schoolboy level.

It was an incredibly exciting time but also totally unique. There's me, with no real link to the school, allowed to take pupils across from Moss Side to Ashton using the school bus. Obviously that wouldn't happen these days, but back then there was a great deal of trust put in me and I like to think that everybody involved benefited from it. Some of those lads still come to see me, decades on, and that means as much to me as any feedback I've had from anybody I've coached.

I took on more and more. I took on further coaching in football, athletics and netball within the extremely busy programme I was running for schools. Amid all this, I ended up having a boxing match with an amateur boxer – just as a demonstration bout – and from that a boxing club arose within our gym. I had the lads build a boxing ring, we got a grant for equipment from Tameside Sports Association and I ran that for 14 years, along with a basketball team and the weightlifting team in which Mark was now a star.

His ability and desire to succeed spearheaded the entire group, and all his team-mates were equally dedicated. We won countless national awards, competitions and trophies in weightlifting, and enjoyed local success in basketball and football.

As the profile of our various teams and clubs grew, I was approached by a member of the Manchester Sports Development Unit, who offered me a role working with mentally and physically handicapped people. While I had no experience whatsoever in that field of coaching, they asked if I could adapt to help people who were missing out on very necessary development. How could I say no to that? I worked with them for about 18 months, which was an extremely emotional undertaking and I needed to really develop my multitasking capabilities to a good level, as the group kept growing each week and all their disabilities were different. That was a major challenge. I was helped by a lot of support workers, but it was up to me to see the way forward for them. I tried my best and had some success. It's a hard field in which to measure success, but I took comfort in the fact that I was later referred to, by one of the MSDU staff, as the senior mental and physical handicapped specialist for Greater Manchester.

That role just stacked up on everything else, including repainting and repointing the entire converted cotton mill in which Olympic sat. I'd often end up stopping through sheer exhaustion in the early hours of the morning, basically sleep in the comfiest spot I could find at the mill, then wake up a few hours later and do it all again. It wasn't a sustainable lifestyle, as I soon found.

My work with the disabled kids took place at Belle Vue sports centre. One particularly hot summer's morning, I arrived about half-an-hour before the session was due to start, having already been around junior and infant schools in the area teaching weightlifting that morning. Everywhere I went, I was loading and unloading a trailer full of the equipment I needed for the various coaching gigs, which was as arduous as it sounds. As I started unloading at Belle Vue, I felt an unbelievable pain snaking through my stomach. I'd had slight pains for a while and ignored them, but this knocked me to the floor. I managed to literally crawl to the toilet, thinking that it was to do with my bowels and something I'd eaten, but when I sat there, I realised it was something far worse.

I have to get home. That was all I could think.

I somehow got back to the car, opened the back door, sagged across the back seat and just passed out. A passer-by woke me up to check if I was ok. I've no idea why, but I just lied and said I was tired. As soon as he left, I got in the front seat, wound it right down so I was leaning back but just about able to see the road. I lived five miles away, but a voice in my head kept saying: "I must get home, I must get home."

I don't remember the journey. Not a bit of it. It's probably confined to one of the darker corners of my mind, as I was in so much pain. I do, however, remember crawling up the stairs at my house and trying to shout to Sue to call an ambulance. I lay on the bed for, I think, around 11 hours before the ambulance arrived.

They quickly got to the bottom of what was happening. My appendix had burst.

I was rushed to Tameside General Hospital and went straight down into surgery.

When I came to, the doctor who had operated on me said that they basically had to take out my insides, wash them down and put everything back in again. He was smiling. I wasn't – my eyes nearly popped out of my head!

"Normally," he said, "we would have cut someone right down the centre of your belly, but we decided to do it at your side to hide the scar from looking too bad, since you obviously work out a lot."

I was in hospital for 13 days in total, during which time I was on a lot of painkillers. Drifting in and out of consciousness, I had a moment of clarity. Despite coaching so many different sports and having a very rounded overview of fitness, I'd failed to heed one key lesson: I was overloading myself. If one of my athletes had done that with a barbell, I'd have gone berserk at them.

I realised I needed to change my working life.

CHAPTER 3

Destiny Calling?

*"I've just turned down Man United, I thought.
What the hell have I done?"*

Mark and his friends ran the gym for three months whilst I recovered from the operation.

Having seen and felt the impact of overdoing things, I limped back into coaching fairly gingerly. In some respects, I picked up where I left off, but there were other things I had to leave behind. I left my electrical engineering job and took on the gym and my coaching roles full-time, with a small nutrition and supplement shop in Ashton.

One new venture which I enjoyed greatly came when I was asked to teach young adults to coach. This I found quite easy because I was already keen to explain everything in detail to the athletes I was coaching, so that they understood what they were doing in enough detail to pass on that knowledge to somebody else. From my experience, you always end up with a better athlete when they essentially become part-time coaches for you.

As my career developed, I would always give responsibility to my athletes by having them coach youngsters in the gym. This method works wonders. Coaching others in what you are trying hard to learn has a massive effect on your own perception of yourself, especially when it comes to your confidence.

. Back then, I built a training programme of easy exercises with simple instructions and with its simplicity came the ability to teach others. After that, it became a case of just extending the training to increase the learning. The programme was very successful and the following year one of the biggest colleges in Europe, Openshaw Technical College, asked me to teach a very large group of adults how to coach. I was initially resistant because, as I told them, I was a coach, not a form-filler or a lecturer. They persuaded me and I took on the role. At the same time, I wrote a power development programme for Manchester Schools' Sports Development department and I coached the Great Britain lacrosse team ahead of the 1996 Olympic Games.

Having got back to full fitness and with my career now dedicated to something that felt incredibly worthwhile, I felt good about life. My mood was certainly helped by the fact that the kids were doing so well. Mark was representing Great Britain in weightlifting, travelling to – and often winning – championships all over the place. He competed at the European and World Championships.

Michael also had an unbelievable development. He was playing well for his football team, Droylsden Boys, but he was 15 and hadn't even been scouted by a non-league team when, after one particular game, he was approached by Brian Poole, who invited him for a trial at Manchester United. Brian was a scout for the club and he saw what an incredibly strong, fit lad Michael was. He was a decent player too, so Brian obviously recognised that there was a lot for them to work with. "I haven't seen that much of him, but there's just something about him," were Brian's exact words. I always believed Michael had something special and, for me, that was his determination to do the best he could.

Brian had been sent out by Dave Bushell, coach of United's Under-16s, to find a centre-back because his group had just lost one of their starting defenders to injury. Even though Michael was a central midfielder at the time, Dave agreed to give him a trial at centre-back in the Under-16s. Once that door was open, there was no way Michael was going to pass up the opportunity. The trial game was at Blackpool and I'll never forget that day. It was as if there were two or three of him. He scored a goal, made a goal-saving block, took corners, free-kicks, throw-ins and even goal-kicks. Everything he could do in the game, he did. That convinced Dave to extend his trial and, within two months, they gave Michael a contract and suddenly he was on the path to United's first team.

Everything happened then. Michael landed a clothing contract with adidas, who invited him in to visit and gave us all gear, including new weightlifting shoes for Mark. We got thousands of pounds of gear. Sue didn't work, so I was a dad with no money, running the gym and maintaining the mill around the clock, feeding five kids, and suddenly we had all this. The kids were the best dressed around – all in sportswear, mind – but we suddenly had clothes. It's amazing, crazy what happened for us.

It carried on, too. Over the next couple of years, Michael was in the Under-18s team that won the FA Youth Cup in 1995, then he stepped up to the first team and made a few senior appearances during the 1996/97 season. He was making such an impression behind the scenes at United because of his unbelievable fitness and power for such a young, relatively small lad, that they started sniffing around his brother, Steven.

Steve worked really hard on all aspects of sport. He was a British schoolboy weightlifting champion three years in a row, a basketball player, a sprinter, a javelin thrower at the highest schoolboy level and when it came to football, he was very decent but he didn't actually enjoy the sport in comparison to the others. Nevertheless, when United offered him a contract, he was happy enough to accept their offer!

Since I had two sons on their books, both of whom were among the best athletes at the club, United started looking into my background. Rob Swire, who was just starting up on the club's physiotherapy team at the time, came to meet me at Olympic. I showed him around and explained the theories behind what I was doing, including plyometrics. I didn't think too much of his visit and just put it down to professional curiosity on his part.

Not long after that, one day in early 1998, the phone rang.

It was Brian Kidd. Alex Ferguson's assistant manager. The same Brian Kidd who had scored for United in the 1968 European Cup final. I'm fortunate enough to remember England winning the World Cup in 1966, but the outstanding footballing memory of my youth – indeed, my whole time as a United fan – was that win over Benfica. Suddenly, I had one of the goalscorers from that night calling me up, out of the blue.

"I've been watching your Michael and Steven, and I've heard about Mark," he said. "I've spoken to Rob and some of the other coaches, and we'd like you to come in and coach plyometrics, because we've heard all about it and we think that can make a difference to us."

"That's fantastic, Brian. Would I be coaching the schoolboys or the youth team lads?"

"No. The first team."

"The first team? No, I can't do that. That's how you get injuries; trying new techniques with older players like Schmeichel or Pallister who haven't done that before. It's very specific training and it will produce injuries when used on those athletes."

"No, no. You'll be alright. Just come in and I'll take responsibility."

"Brian, you're telling me that you'll take responsibility for something that you've had no contact with before. I've had experience in plyometrics and it's a major reason all my athletes do well. But they're all young, I've not got any older ones so I can't do that with your players."

The line went dead.

I've just turned down Man United, I thought. *What the hell have I done?*

Now, this is 100 percent true. More than once, long before Michael signed on as a player, I had actually dreamed of working at United. I woke up after truly vivid dreams of working there, studying the players and coaching them. In the space of maybe 60 seconds on the phone, I'd turned down the chance to literally turn my dreams into reality.

Facepalm, as my grandkids would say.

At times over the coming days, weeks, months, I tried to justify it to myself because, by that stage, I had already spent a fair amount of time criticising United for the way they were treating our Michael.

Obviously, despite being a coach, you can't help but see things from a father's perspective, so when Michael wasn't being given – in my opinion – enough opportunities to prove himself and unseat Gary Neville as starting right-back, I used to slate United to anyone who would listen. I always thought Michael would get through and do well, and obviously what I envisaged happening for him wasn't happening. Even though I'd been a United fan all my life, a part of me was growing to hate the club for not giving my son more opportunities.

So, working for them may have been my dream job, but focusing on their part in my lad's struggles allowed me to make peace with inadvertently turning it down. Then – call it fate, a higher power, whatever your beliefs are – later that year, Brian Kidd left to manage Blackburn Rovers. A few months later, at the end of the 1998/99 season, he recruited United's head physio, Dave Fevre, and that meant he needed replacing. Alex Ferguson plumped for Rob Swire, who had been the first to recommend me.

That appointment would prove to be instrumental in my career trajectory thereafter. Not that I had any clue at that exact time, since I had other issues going on in my life.

CHAPTER 4

Together But Apart

"When everyone else in Greater Manchester and millions of people around the world were celebrating Ole Gunnar Solskjaer's Treble-winning goal, I was having a blazing row which marked the end of my marriage."

Anybody with the faintest affiliation with Manchester United knows the significance of 26 May 1999. It was probably the greatest night in the history of the club; the night that they faced Bayern Munich in the Champions League final and were 1-0 down as stoppage time began. By the time those three minutes were up, they'd done something that no other team in the history of English football had done: they'd won the Treble.

My highlight of supporting United as a kid was the 1968 European Cup final as a 10-year-old. I was old enough to appreciate that it was a huge game and winning it was a massive deal, but I maybe didn't quite grasp the significance of the journey to that point. I was born late in 1957, the year before the Munich air disaster, so Matt Busby had been rebuilding the club for the entire decade that I'd been alive, and the culmination was beating Benfica at Wembley to become the first English champions of Europe.

Fast forward to 1999, and I was well aware of the significance of what Alex Ferguson was in the middle of achieving. He'd already ended the 26-year wait to be league champions and United were the dominant force in England, but the 31-year wait to be European champions was his next problem to solve. When United won the final in 1999, having already won the Premier League and FA Cup, the club made history as England's first-ever Treble winners.

Michael was around the squad at that stage, but he was on the periphery and wasn't in the travelling party, so he was in Ashton with me and the rest of the family on the day of the game. Although there was always the chance I'd be working late because Olympic closed at 9pm, I was looking forward to watching the game.

Apart from Shaun, who was five or six at the time, everyone else was going to the pub to watch the final. During the evening, the other kids came to the gym and between them asked me if they could borrow my car. I absent-mindedly agreed and they took my car keys – house keys included – so, when I ended up finishing in the gym at 9pm, my plans to watch the second half were scuppered because I had to walk home. By the time I got back and couldn't get in, Shaun was cold and needed shelter so I had to knock on at one of the neighbours' houses to see if he could go in there and keep warm while I went about trying to track everyone down. No house keys, no car, no final, no nothing.

The first person back after the final whistle was Sue and we had a blazing row where everything came to a head.

We'd fought more and more over the years and a fair bit of resentment had crept into the relationship.

Like all young love, we'd started off in a whirlwind and we'd not so much gone down the well-trodden path as hijacked a bullet train and careered madly down it. I know people in their 20s and 30s now who have one foot in a relationship and rent a flat together. By the time Sue and I hit 30, we'd been married homeowners for over a decade and had a litter of kids. I recognise that the world has changed now and what we did was just the done thing back then, but in retrospect we definitely crammed in a lot early on.

Nevertheless, initially there was good balance to the relationship. Sue was a smoker and, when we were 18, we worked out how much it was costing Sue to smoke and we agreed that I should buy a guitar that matched the money she was spending on cigarettes.

Kids change relationships. That's just a fact of life. Sometimes for better, sometimes for worse. It depends on how you absorb the demands and responsibilities of parenthood. Sue gave up full-time work when Michael was born, later taking on a part-time role in a launderette, while I still had my dreams of making it in music. One day, I was supposed to be watching Michael when he was 18 months old, but instead I was focusing on trying to play a piece and he made a mess on the floor when I wasn't watching. I shouted, he started crying and just thought to myself: *You rotten shit*. He was such a nice kid and I'd shouted at him when it was my fault for not watching him properly.

It started to melt me into how much time I was spending practising and also at the same time I was going out doing gigs and probably wasn't spending enough time at home. I had my job as an electrical fitter at Norweb, I had my music dreams and I'd also started going to the gym at that stage. I wanted to be a rock guitarist, wanted to look the part, play the part, but looking back I was probably very, very selfish. I was very me, me, me, but I'd looked past that and justified it to myself because I was the main breadwinner. I went to work and worked hard to pay for everything.

As Michael started growing up and suddenly developed his interest in *Monkey* and martial arts, I developed more of an interest in the training than the guitar. Suddenly I was taking him to football, taekwondo and other activities, then Mark was born, Steven was born, Mandy was born, Shaun was born. During that timeframe I probably became obsessed with the kids and coaching them. I was always coaching, getting qualifications, taking the kids to different sporting events and I know that Sue, over the years, felt that she'd been left alone in the house.

When I opened up Olympic, she didn't want to be a part of it. When I packed in my job at Norweb aged 29 to go full-time with the gym and the shop, she said it was the stupidest move I'd ever make. My dad died earlier that year and he'd been in the job most of his life, so I made the decision to get out of there because I hated it and I feared that I'd be there for the rest of my life.

From being 30 to 41, I was out of the house a lot. Over that period of time Sue got bored and upset and felt as though we had all these kids and had this massive family, but we were never actually together. I might be off with one of them at an event or a game, leaving the other four with her, then I'd come back and have three and she'd have two, or I'd have all five of them at the gym and so on. Whatever the configurations, the point was that we were always apart. Together but apart. She kept saying to me bit by bit that she was sick of living that way, especially after I'd left Norweb – which I thought was the decision that set me free – so we had disagreements on that.

Things were very passionate and would often get heated. She asked me to move out three times, but then asked me to come back three times as well. I went along with it each time but, as you can imagine, that kind of yo-yoing takes an emotional toll and I didn't like the way I was treated for, in my eyes, working hard for the family unit and doing everything I could to give the kids the best possible chance of having extraordinary lives.

When I came back the third time, I told Sue that the next time she asked me to leave, I'd be gone for good. That was in late 1998. So, when everyone else in Greater Manchester and millions of people around the world were celebrating Ole Gunnar Solskjaer's Treble-winning goal, I was in the middle of a blazing row which marked the end of my marriage.

I told Sue I was sick of being treated that way. I felt I was working really hard for the family without being appreciated, constantly being pushed away and pulled back. She left the house that night, I didn't chase after her because I was sick of the situation, and after a while she asked me to leave so that she could move back in.

We had a big meeting at the family house where I made it clear that if I left, I wouldn't be coming back. She said that was fine because she'd had enough anyway. She was tired of me not doing various things, so she was sick of the situation too. I just left. There was no big legal wrangle, I just told her that she could have the house and I'd have the gym, so I went and lived there and just worked myself into the ground so that I could continue paying off their house for them. I went back every single day and took Shaun to school up to the point that, at 14, he told me I was embarrassing him.

Obviously when you go through something like that, it's inevitable that you reflect on it and dwell on what you might have done differently. A lot of time has passed. The kids grew up and left, Sue's still living in the house with her new partner and I think she's a lot happier than she was with me. We speak now and then, not often, and I feel really sad about it when I look back. I can say with a totally clear conscience that I worked as hard as I could to provide for the family.

The kids never wanted for anything because I made sure they had everything. They weren't spoiled with material things; if anything they were spoiled with the opportunities they had. Sue, though, didn't get enough attention from me and I can see that now. I can only agree with her complaints about the marriage. I dedicated myself to parenting, coaching and teaching, but I just couldn't teach myself to be a good husband.

I have to add, though, that – with the benefit of hindsight – leaving the job at Norweb didn't turn out to be the biggest mistake ever. Sue had said I was walking away from a job for life, but most of the people I knew left the industry before they retired, and coaching didn't just end up being my career – all five of our kids now do my job. They all earn their living by doing what I was doing. We learnt together as father and children. We carved a new path together. We were all into sport, all had great opportunities, so I think I made the right choice. I wouldn't be writing this if I didn't.

The chances that have been presented to me over the

years have been tremendous, and I like to think I've taken advantage of the opportunities that people have given me. I think I've done the right thing. There are obviously parts of me that are missing, but you can't have it all. My parenting and professional career were extreme, and the price for that was my first marriage.

I can look back now as an old fella and reflect calmly on the choices I've made, of course, but at the time I had quite a few years of living alone at the gym where I had to wrangle with all kinds of concerns about what a state of flux things were suddenly in. At the start of the Treble season, I'd been in a steady job with a wife and a family home. Shortly after it, I was single and living alone in a cold, sweaty gym where I worked every available hour.

Towards the end of United's next season, though, I was handed a most unexpected opportunity. While the Treble campaign had been ongoing, the club were in the midst of moving from their original training ground at the Cliff to a brand-new, state-of-the-art facility at Carrington, where they'd had a gym built. They were looking for someone who could bring a new dimension to the training of the Academy players, while Alex Ferguson – Sir Alex within a few weeks – was determined to fill the new facility with the best players and staff available.

Rob Swire came to me in early 2000 and offered me the job of running it.

In one of my increasingly terse conversations with Sue, she made it clear that, having slagged United off for Michael's lack of opportunities, taking the job would make me a hypocrite.

This time, I accepted. Given the second chance to join Manchester United, I couldn't say no.

CHAPTER 5

Missing Pieces

"We don't know what you're doing or how you do it. Just go and do it. As long as there aren't any players getting injured."

On my first day at Carrington in March 2000, Rob Swire met me in reception and took me over to the Academy building where I'd soon be working with United's youth team.

I met with their coaches, Dave Williams and Neil Bailey, and talked to them. After Rob had introduced us, they got straight down to business.

"So, what are you going to do, then?"

I knew exactly what I was going to do, because it was all that I did. Boxing, weightlifting, strength training. That would give the young lads a strength element, a power element, but also the explosive power element of boxing, as well as quite advanced plyometrics targeting the upper body and lower body.

It wasn't something I'd learnt from somebody else; you couldn't go and find clips on YouTube. Michael used to run, box, lift weights, and plyometrics had become something that I'd really taken to heart after reading an article about the basics of it, so I took it and developed the idea of advanced plyometrics. Then I melded them all together into this routine. To this day, my type of training isn't a series of individual exercises, it's a combination of lots of exercises. Now I call it splice training.

After I'd explained what I was going to do, Rob said: "We don't know what you're doing or how you do it. Just go and do it. As long as there aren't any players getting injured."

That was the difference. The coaches at Carrington had never seen anything like it before. Neither had the players.

Apart from Steven.

Steven wasn't a footballer. He was an athlete who played football. He played games with his brothers and his brothers' mates, who were around three to six years older, so he was always learning to compete against somebody he shouldn't really be able to compete against. It was his competitive nature that allowed him to break school records in sprinting, shot put and so on. He didn't like weightlifting, but he did it because he won all the time because I'd taught him. It was too easy for him when he was competing with his own age group. I'd already taught him in school when I'd gone in at Audenshaw and he was by far the best.

I'd made most of my rookie coaching mistakes on Michael and Mark, so Steven got the best of me. He was more free-spirited. He could go and do whatever he wanted without me focusing him on anything in particular. He won the British Championships of weightlifting three years in a row despite virtually doing about 15-30 weightlifting sessions per year and not really concentrating on it. He'd play basketball with Mark, football with Michael, and the lads who played basketball against him said he was virtually able to play on his own against a team, he was that good. All this time he was spending across various sports meant that he was doing more hours than anybody else. The journalist Malcolm Gladwell famously theorised that you need 10,000 hours of practice at something to master it, which would basically equate to three hours per day for nine years or so. Whether that rule is true or not, Steven was playing sport for more than that each day. Probably three hours a day in the week and more than double that on Saturday and Sunday.

So, he was an unbelievable sportsman accustomed to thriving in groups where he should have been inferior. On my first day at United, he was number one in the room. Alan Tate, who played centre-back with Steven and went on to have a good career at Swansea City, was in the group. He and the other footballers, like Danny Nardiello, all looked shocking when they tried to do the training I was setting them. They couldn't keep up with Steven at all. He looked like a goliath, a pure athlete.

In some ways, that might have been difficult for him because he was so good as an athlete, but when it came onto the football pitch, he felt exposed. He knew he wasn't as good at football as the lads around him, many of whom had already played for England's youth teams. That, I think, tainted the ability he'd built of playing against older lads. Suddenly he was in his own age group with lads that he was athletically far better than, but skilfully inferior to. On the pitch you could see who had done all their training in football. Steven's was spread across all kinds of sports.

That was one of the big factors in why I train like I do today. You can train strength, speed, power, all these things, but on the football pitch there has to be a skill element. There has to be skill involved in what you're doing, and the art is in how you place those skills into the drills that you do. Each sport has to have the skill factor, whether it's football, cricket or curling. You can be as athletic as you want around the periphery, but if you don't have the specific skills for that sport, you're going to come up short.

I was very aware of that because Michael and Steven had gone in as athletes who could play football, and when you're there watching as a parent – before I took the job – you can see what they're missing.

So, when I first took the job at United, the players I worked with were telling me what they needed to work on. I could reason that out because my lads were so good athletically, but I could see that there were pieces missing when they played football. You're forever searching for pieces to fill in the whole. So, when a player sits down with you – whether it's Alan Tate, Danny Nardiello or Ryan Giggs, it's not rocket science. You find out what he needs himself, and each one of those young lads would tell you what they needed.

I noticed that the kids also got their information from their parents. They know in their own minds some of the things that they're lacking, but parents were also telling their kids to ask me about various aspects of their game. I see kids rowing with their parents all the time now, but the truly intelligent kids are the ones who listen to their parents, see that their parents' ideas differ to theirs, and then put them together with their own ideas. The kids who progress well in sport very often have really solid relationships with their parents over the course of their career. If I'm given that internal knowledge of a family trying to get their son to the highest level, they'll put their heart and soul into it. When you've got three people

– two parents and the child – looking at a subject together, especially on the emotive levels of trying to be a footballer, you've suddenly got a force there.

* * *

Obviously, I had a discussion with my own kids before I took the job at United. Michael knew I'd be seeing him around Carrington, Steven knew I'd be training him alongside his team-mates, but it honestly wasn't a big concern for them because there had been a lot of previous experience in that field. When they were going into school, their dad turned up teaching in the school. When they joined a football team, their dad turned up coaching, just as he did when they joined athletics teams, basketball teams, weightlifting teams and so on. I was around their lives all the time.

All the while, they recognised what they were getting, that their mates wanted what they were getting, so I don't think they were ever embarrassed that their dad was always around them. It was just what they were used to. It had been going on their whole lives and they were seeing success from it. Michael was around the first-team squad, Steven was in the youth team, Mark was going around the world in weightlifting, and naturally there's a reason for those things happening. Don't get me wrong, I'm sure I embarrassed all five of my kids at different times and in different ways, but they were used to me doing what I did in a coaching capacity, so why would they be worried at all?

When I saw them around Carrington, I wouldn't spend any time conversing with them. I'd let on, of course, but I always just made a point of keeping moving. That was the best way to keep out from under people's feet. I always remember Albert Morgan, the kitman, on my first pre-season tour with the first team, came over to me and said: "I've been watching you. When we have new people come around the first team, they want to be there all the time, listening to everything, being involved in everything, but you know how to get out of the way and that's really helpful. You do your bit and get out of the way."

That comes from being with the kids in their school, in their football team, their basketball team, their weightlifting team. You do your bit and get out of the way because you don't want to embarrass your kids, so they were all key things. If you go on the tour and you're a pain in the arse, you don't go on tour again. I was very fortunate in that sense that I had practice of being around teams and clubs before I came in at United. I had a reasonable knowledge of it because I'd been schooled in the way of good athletes.

The young lads at United, though, were a properly talented bunch of footballers. They may not have gotten too many into the first team from that crop, but that's because the standard was so high. It was virtually impossible to break into that team during that time. They'd just won the Treble, after all. So, while I went in there with one eye on watching what Steven could do compared with what the top players could do, I was acutely aware of the professional privilege of working with the best young players around.

I'd go into Carrington twice a week at first. There were maybe 25 to 30 players between the first and second years, and I had to train all of them. Then, when the coaching staff started noticing how well that was going, there was more interest. Tony Whelan, a diamond of a guy and a very well respected coach in the Academy who looked after the really young lads, straight away saw the benefits and said: "Hey, what about my boys?"

I started getting pulled over the place to help this person and that person.

And one very important person.

CHAPTER 6

The Skipper

"So there we were, out on the pitch on a hot summer's day at Carrington, with all the players gathered around as first Roy Keane then Wes Brown boxed through two rounds with me."

The most important period of my career began three months after I had started working with United's youth team.

Rob Swire told me that Roy Keane had injured his knee and he asked me to come to Carrington and spend some time with him in the summer of 2000. At that stage, Roy was a key part of the team, in his omnipresent pomp around the turn of the millennium and it was imperative to the team's ambitions that he was absolutely in the right condition.

He was the captain, the engine, the heartbeat of a team which had conquered England, Europe and the world in the previous year. He'd also had his problems with his knees before, having injured his anterior cruciate ligament in 1997, and this latest bout of trouble followed on from niggles he'd had with his ankle and hamstring. Not only was it a massive shock to my system to be asked to work with him so early in my career at United, but there was enormous pressure to ensure that he was fit and functional in double-quick time. I'll always remember the first time I met Roy. You don't forget characters like him. I walked into the gym at Carrington, where Rob had warmed him up so that he was ready to jump straight into a session with me. I wasn't ready for that. They asked me what I was going to do and I thought for a second, before asking Roy: "Do you sup tea?"

A pause, while the first signs of disdain began to creep on to his face.

"What?"

"Tea. Do you drink tea?"

"Yeah. Why?"

He was indulging me, but warily.

"Because we're going to go up to the canteen, have a brew and talk through what you need," I explained. "There's no way we can properly start working together until we know a bit about each other and I know what you want and need from me."

We had to work out where to start, so we went for a brew and I asked him to tell me about himself and his training methods so I could look at what he might need from a gym. Roy talked to me for around an hour about his life, what he had been through, what he liked doing and what he didn't like doing and it gave me a massive opportunity to learn and understand from a bona fide football legend.

The first thing he talked about was boxing, and at the time I'd had Olympic Boxing Club for about 12 years, so we inevitably got talking in detail about that. He recalled how he had four amateur fights and he said he had won them all. I said: "Well, obviously we're going to have some boxing in your training so I'll see if that's true or not," and I just looked him in the eye, he looked back and we both knew that we had to prove ourselves to each other. It wasn't just about me proving myself to him. And do you really think Roy Keane was going to duck any kind of challenge, especially one like that?

At first we had to do other work around his injury, so we could only talk about boxing and share stories of it but, sure enough, when the time came, we got to work with the pads and I could tell that Roy had boxed before. You can tell from the way someone stands, the way they move, the way they punch, and he had definitely thrown some punches before. We built up a relationship over the summer, and after a few sessions Roy was showing fantastic aggression and reactions. The other players began filtering back for pre-season and word soon got round that Roy was boxing, so before long they were all hanging around and watching his sessions.

Having Roy Keane boxing and all these players watching from the periphery was new territory for me, and it turned out it was for them too, as they'd barely done any work with weights outside rehabilitation. So, with Rob's blessing, I introduced a training session, just to see what they could do, using press-ups, chin-ups, dips, squats and the like, and at the end we had boxing for football specificity. As an introduction, I told them that Roy and I would do some boxing, and I also did a session with Wes Brown. So there we were, out on the pitch on a hot summer's day at Carrington, with all the players gathered around as first Roy, then Wes boxed through two rounds with me.

As a physical specimen, Wes was fantastic – believe me, you want to hold the pads while he boxes, it bloody hurts – but all his strength was in his lower body. He couldn't do a single chin-up, but that didn't matter with the pads. You don't need upper body strength; just hip power and the ability to let your arm lock out. It's all in the hips, not the arms, so Wes was really good at boxing. They both were.

Now, these guys were used to playing in front of thousands of fans every week, knowing that their every kick was being watched on television by millions of people around the world, but when you get all their team-mates together then that's different pressure altogether. Roy and Wes were excellent under pressure that day – really powerful, really quick – and they each got an amazing standing ovation from all the lads. I could see that Roy was proud as punch, and that's what made our relationship: the fact that the work he'd done with me had made him look good in front of all his team-mates. From there we went on to have a fantastic working relationship.

Training Roy was very, very easy because I had an understanding of him and he also knew a little bit about me from our initial chat. He knew I was prepared to listen to him, he knew I was prepared to understand what he wanted, and to try and make sure that he got all the bits of training that he thought was necessary for him to be effective on the pitch.

Roy would wind me up until I told him to shut up. He encouraged me to have a go at him; he liked to stimulate aggression from everyone around him and that made him successful. We would push each other – I'll always remember him approaching me in the Carrington gym one day, when we were trialling a new exercise, and saying: "Mr Clegg, you use me in the gym like I'm a crash test dummy for your development." I replied: "Roy, you are benefiting from cutting edge revelations, so shut your mouth and do it!" He did it, of course, because he always did what he had to do in order to improve.

On a personal level, it's impossible to understate the importance of having Roy buy into my training methods. Not only was it tremendous validation to have a top-level player believing in what I was saying, but also Roy was extraordinarily influential within the dressing room. He was the definition of a captain. He demanded the best of himself and everybody around him, and his incessant drive helped propel everybody in the vicinity. If you gave your all then you were fine, but if you didn't then he would let you know about it, and nobody wanted to be on the wrong side of Roy.

He would tell you straight if you were letting yourself or the team down, and he more than any other player was responsible for dragging up the standards that were demanded across the club.

There's no disputing that Roy is a fiercely driven competitor – he's proud to admit it – but the public perception of him couldn't be further removed from the man himself. What company he is. A sharp, intelligent, funny character who doesn't suffer fools and is simply very wary of who he should trust. He has more levels of grey matter than he was ever renowned for. When you meet him for the first time you can feel his eyes boring into you, but if he trusts what he sees and you strike up a good relationship with him, then he is a wonderful man to know.

Years later, after I had left United, I worked with Warrington Wolves to help prepare them during their 2012 Super League campaign. The sessions went really well, the lads were completely engaged and they made it to the final, losing narrowly to Leeds Rhinos at Old Trafford, but as part of that work I asked Roy if he would come along to speak to the group. He agreed without hesitation and they were all absolutely transfixed, hanging on his every word. Some enormous physical specimens, guys who could dominate a room themselves, were absolutely silent as he spoke – you could feel the respect they had for him.

Tony Smith, Wolves' head coach, later said that everybody was absolutely blown away by Roy's honesty and his stories. He had no need to go along and help them out, but he did it and, like he did with everything, he put his all into it and got fantastic results.

I also occasionally trained Roy after his retirement when his schedule permitted it, and nobody will be surprised to learn that he was exactly as driven then as he was in his prime as a player. When you're such a fierce competitor, that drive never leaves you. When he's old and grey, Roy will be the nursing home's bingo champion, checkers champion and first in the canteen queue. Back in the summer of 2000, however, he was just a world-class footballer. Moreover, on a personal level, he was an important ally as I set off down an exciting new career path.

CHAPTER 7

Tough Glove

"You don't tend to think of footballers in terms of smashing somebody in the face, but if you get them in the right zone with the boxing then they become very, very aggressive and competitive."

So, why boxing?

It's quite incongruous that the crucial introductory phase of my work with a football club owed so much to another sport altogether – and one without teams or a ball, at that – but boxing had played a major part in my coaching career to that point. It has done ever since I first pulled on a pair of pads and still does to this very day.

Growing up, I always loved watching boxing on television. My dad was a huge Muhammad Ali fan, so I was too. Later, I loved Mike Tyson, but not before the entire family had become huge fans of the movie *Rocky* when it came out in 1976. Now, the thing about *Rocky* is that it used boxing to make its point, but really it could have been about any sport. It was an ingenious way for Sylvester Stallone to conjure up the emotion of passion.

In the film, Stallone was utilising his heart, not his brain. This boxer starts off his career, wins some fights, loses some fights, gets pretty brain-dead along the way, but little things are working for him, things that keep him going even though he should really have packed in ages ago, and then he gets the biggest chance in the world, to fight Apollo Creed, and he can either take it or not take it. Rocky decides to take this chance. My apologies if this is spoiling the movie, by the way, but I just can't imagine a world in which anybody hasn't seen *Rocky*, so I feel like I'm on safe ground.

The whole story is about his heart adjusting to what's happening in his life and making what turn out to be the right decisions. It's all about feelings. What Stallone does in that film is really get to the crux of what your feelings do for you. You have so much information in your brain, but it's vastly inferior to your heart in terms of making decisions about what you want and what you do.

Rocky Balboa was a boxer, but the movie could have been about an ice hockey player, someone going to the moon or becoming the world's best beekeeper – or anything, really. The aim was to tug at your heartstrings and rouse your passion, so boxing was a fantastic choice with which to do that. Once you start to emote and become passionate, that's why you can gain so much energy and utilise it to do what you really want to do.

Passion and boxing are firmly interlinked. When I think back to the origins of my first boxing club, emotion played a huge part in its formation. When I partook in the charity boxing bout, long before I joined United, my memories are very clear. Firstly, I've never felt such heat in all my life. It was under lights in mid-July in this packed Tameside theatre in Ashton-under-Lyne and it was absolutely sweltering. Secondly, the noise of the crowd has always stayed with me. It was a healthy mixture of kids taking the piss out of the old fella getting his brain smashed out and some people encouraging the old fella because they didn't want to witness a murder that night. All of that gave rise to a lot of passion; I could virtually feel it in the air while blow after blow rained down upon me.

When you raise that passion, people react. Everyone was coming up to me afterwards and saying how much fun they'd had. On that wave of emotion, my first boxing club was born and that contributed to me picking up years of sparring experience before I joined United.

My career path had already flitted from Olympic lifting to plyometrics, then boxing came into the equation, so the focus had gone from lower body to upper body and back to lower. With boxing, the obvious action is in the arms, so it's easy to assume that the sport is all about the upper body. It's not. The force starts from the ground up and your arms coming out are just the end point – a fist hitting someone's face is essentially the same as the football being kicked into the goal.

When I first started work at United, I had the Under-18s doing weightlifting, plyometrics and boxing alongside their football training. Then, when I sat down to do that first consultation with Roy, there was no hook for me with weights or plyometrics because he'd had no experience of either. Boxing, however, gave us a starting point.

We went down into the gym, started applying moves for his knee and then, once the rehab was over, started applying boxing principles. It really lifted the whole place. A few weeks after that sparring session with Roy and Wes in front of the whole squad, Steve McClaren, assistant manager at the time, said to me: "You've come in here and everyone wants to work with you." The players were practically lining up to have a go with the pads. Phil Neville was next to do a bit, Ryan Giggs would come in and want a go, then Paul Scholes, and it built up. And it comes from that emotion of boxing.

With boxing, I can really get into people's minds. I've got the focus mitts, I'm getting them to throw punches and just for instance I can say: "Come on you pussy, put some bloody power into that punch," and then they emote, try to hit you harder and become more aggressive. It's rudimentary psychology, but it works. Now I'd been doing that with kids for years – not always calling them pussies, I should stress – but I hadn't really joined the dots and recognised what was happening. I'd seen how much more passionate my own kids had become through boxing, but I didn't make the connection until I got to United that boxing was a great way of cultivating emotion in athletes.

I learned by sparring with those players that really good athletes are really good athletes for more than one reason. David Beckham wasn't just good at pinpoint deliveries or shooting from distance; within him there was a massive amount of passion which he used on the field and you could provoke it to the surface by putting a pair of sparring gloves on him. You don't tend to think of footballers in terms of smashing somebody in the face, but if you get them in the right zone with the boxing then they become very, very aggressive and competitive.

Wes was a big, powerful lad and his punches were amazing, whereas Roy was much smaller and slimmer, but the speed of his punches was sensational. So, right from the off, I found myself watching the speed of punches, the power of punches, the ability to move and I was assessing what speeds people could attain. I learned so much about each of those players from the time I spent sparring with them, and not all of it was predictable.

If you compare Wes with Jaap Stam, for example, you'd think that it would be far harder to stop Jaap from punching you, but in fact the opposite was true. Jaap was older and bigger so, as you would expect, his punches were huge. However, they were coming at you with more total force, but at a slower pace, so you're able to manoeuvre yourself to absorb the blow. With Wes, however, you had a young, slim lad who could throw good, powerful punches substantially quicker. So much faster that it was more devastating. If you get someone who's really fast, then you can't manoeuvre yourself into the right position before it hits you, and it bloody hurts. It wears you down faster.

What I did as an assessment over the years was use my hands to feel somebody's punches. I did thousands and thousands of rounds of people throwing punches at me, so you get to feel their power. Over time you learn lessons, one of which was to always expect the unexpected. You'd never, ever think it to look at him, but Chris Eagles was one of the most powerful punchers of the lot. His ability to punch was amazing.

The kid was skinny and always looked pristine. He never had a hair out of place and really took care of the way he looked, so I didn't expect him to have too much interest in boxing at all. If you stuck to stereotypes and preconceptions, you'd think he'd stick to mid-sections and biceps, but little else besides them.

When I felt him punch the pads, I was taken aback at the power and ferocity he could generate, and I put that down to his ability to harness emotion. It wasn't just with the boxing, either. A few years after I first pulled on the pads with Chris, I was in the gym with Ben Foster and John Davin, United's physiotherapist. We'd finished whatever session we were doing and idly chatting about something mundane when the conversation somehow became a contest to see which of us could hit the gym roof with a 10kg medicine ball. None of us could do it.

Eagles marches in, to all intents and purposes just a skinny little wimp, and he hits the roof with his first attempt. He was probably 20kg lighter than Ben, but he just did it at the first attempt and started laughing at us all. Ben was so annoyed, he wanted to rip him apart. This huge, hulking bear of a guy just couldn't believe that skinny little Eagles could do that while he couldn't, but the underdog was able to by harnessing his heart.

Over time, once you've realised the role of pure emotion in these athletes, you see it surfacing all the time and you learn to use it in the gym. The most important thing within their passion is the switch; the feeling that says yes or no to doing something. So, when you take a collection of exercises, whether it's on a bound, laminated folder or scrawled on the back of a napkin, and you take that to your athlete, it's about what passion you can stir within them to give them the drive to get ready for whatever they need to do in their sport.

This is something I've picked up over time. I never went into the United job with a bunch of coaching theories, I was just very deliberate in making sure that I went into it with an open mind. That meant that I had to listen, which is why, after having such a successful consultation with Roy, I had one with every single player at the club so that I could understand what they needed from me and then I could go about working out how to achieve that. To this very day, whenever anybody comes into my gym in Ashton and looks around at the walls and sees the pictures of all the players I've worked with, I tell them the same thing: they are my mentors. Those are the people who taught me how to coach. I wasn't taught by a professor at university, I was taught by the elite athletes who told me what they needed from me in order to become better at what they were doing.

As a coach, you can't make the mistake of thinking you know what somebody needs without asking them. If you are shown a need, there is more chance of you being effective than you showing someone else what they need, or what you believe their needs to be. When Paul Scholes or David Beckham or Gary Neville tell you that they need *this*, you have a collision of hearts where you work together from an emotional place. To really be creative with another person is to understand them, show them the knowledge that you have and see how they can match and be used together as a force.

Two forces together is always going to be more than one force on its own. If you can collide with various members of a squad, then imagine the force you can generate.

CHAPTER 8

Earning Respect

"You have to be so careful about how you treat footballers. Andy Cole is an example of how I got it wrong, but got lucky in the end. With Rio Ferdinand, I managed to get it right at the first attempt – but it was another hairy moment."

In my early days with the first team, it certainly helped my cause to have Roy Keane in my corner. He commanded respect from every single player in that squad, and it was a star-studded group of players at the time.

Although I'd won a big battle in winning Roy over, I still had a lot of work to do because in that environment you constantly have to prove yourself as being worthy of being at Manchester United. The standards were so high that, whatever your job, if you weren't up to it then you were soon found out.

I was the first power development coach in the Premier League. Possibly because of that, and what I was doing was new and unfamiliar to the players, the vast majority of my early time at the club went really well. But, of course, I made mistakes too, and I almost made a very costly one early in my United career. It involved Andy Cole. My relationship with

Andy was curious, because he's one of those players who'd look at you and you could see him thinking: *I'm not sure about this guy.* In the gym I would have players doing circuits: one squatting, one bench pressing and so on, and I'd always be at another station to box with one of them. Now Andy, I think, liked the idea of boxing because he was a bit of a mover. Every time he threw a right cross, however, he'd lean into it but he'd never pull it back. I told the players that they always had to get back in position, so I kept saying to him: "If you throw a punch out, bring it back in and get your position for the next punch."

I used to do three circuits, and one day on the first circuit I said: "Andy, you keep throwing that right cross and leaving yourself there. I could easily hit you, don't do that." Second circuit, he did it again. "Andy, I've told you. Don't leave your head there or I'll hit it in a minute." Of course, this was Andy Cole. How much had he won? How many goals had he scored? He'd been around the block and this was me as a coach in my first year, and this is where I made a really big mistake. Next time around he did it again and I slapped his glove and shouted at him: "You fucking did it again, I'm going to hit you in a minute." He took the gloves off, threw them on the floor and said: "Fuck you, I don't need your fucking boxing."

The rest of the lads were all stood there watching and had seen everything unfold, so after a moment or two I collected myself, shouted for everyone else to carry on and I just tried to get through the rest of the session. To be honest, I was worried. How could I not be? There was an atmosphere for the next few minutes, but I was very fortunate because I think what I did, although stupid, was brave, and while the stupidity led me to lose the faith of a top-quality player, I think the other players recognised I was trying to coach and Andy wasn't listening or buying into what I was saying.

But there was no question that it was a massive mistake on my part, showing total disrespect to a player who deserved better, and it took a long time to turn that mistake around. Andy didn't speak to me for three months. He didn't start again until he was injured and I was doing a session with Jaap Stam, with whom I got on brilliantly well. Jaap was doing a press behind the neck, I was spotting him, and Andy walked in. As Jaap got off the bench, Andy got on, so as normal I just lifted the bar, he pressed it, carried on and got off. He'd not spoken to me since the outburst.

So I said: "Right, Jaap, are we doing some lateral raises?" and he went over and started doing them. Andy came along afterwards and did them as well. The session carried on like this, with Andy doing everything that Jaap had done. Neither of us spoke until, in the end, I said: "Are you alright Andy?"

"Yeah, I'm alright."

"Fucking hell, you've not spoken to me for three months!"

"You don't fucking deserve to be spoken to, you little c***!"

Then after that we got on like a house on fire. This guy had won the Treble, scored so many goals at Newcastle and United, become an absolute hero to United fans, but at that time his career at Old Trafford was just about on the downturn. The club had attempted to sign Ruud van Nistelrooy and were openly going to go back in for him when he had recovered from a serious knee injury.

I think Andy felt within the club that he was not as important, not treated in the manner he was used to and probably my insolence was something he had to rebel against because he felt hurt and annoyed. It taught me a very important lesson about respect for people. I was trying to do my job but I shouldn't have done it at the expense of respecting someone. We get on very well now, but it took a long time to repair the damage done by that misjudgement.

* * *

When dealing with footballers, particularly in the early days of your relationship with them and particularly in front of their team-mates, you have to be so careful about how you treat them. Andy Cole is an example of how I got it wrong, but got lucky in the end. With Rio Ferdinand a couple of years later, I managed to get it right at the first attempt – but it was another hairy moment.

The interesting thing about Rio is his personality. He was an absolutely enormous presence in that group, even in his early days after joining from Leeds in 2002. There were some truly gigantic characters already in that dressing room, and it would have been very intimidating for virtually any newcomer coming into that group of players with the expectation of not only fitting in, but also lifting the collective standard. What Rio had in his favour was that, whilst being a huge guy with a huge talent, he had the character to go with it.

He hadn't been at the club for long, but I'd done some work with him and I already had a sense for his likes and dislikes in the gym. He enjoyed doing upper body work because he was quite strong up there, certainly the strongest we had during my time at the club. One morning, after a match the previous evening in which he hadn't been on top of his game, I felt confident enough to pass comment on his performance.

I asked: "What was up with you last night?"

He was understandably a little shocked and defensive, asking: "What do you mean?"

"Dunno, you just looked a bit off."

"I wasn't."

"I've seen you better."

"I don't know what you're saying."

Now, Rio was a very proud man. I was aware of this, so I left it a few minutes. He was doing some bench work, in my opinion some way short of full throttle, and I went over to him, touched him on the shoulder and said: "You need to put a bit more effort in than that."

He sat up.

"Don't you fucking touch me."

He was sat on the bench, I was stood up, but we were virtually face to face. I'm a ratty little shit and here's this massive guy with a furious look on his face, and his face was virtually touching mine.

It was a sweet moment in time, and I always talk to athletes about those very instants because that is the kind of moment when things can go very, very right or very, very wrong. Fortunately for me, it swung the way of the former.

I said: "Why, what are you going to do about it?"

And this big smile crept across his face and he said: "You fucking get me, you do," and that was it. If I'd taken the other option – which would've been so easy to do – and backed down, especially to a new person coming in, and one with such an influential personality, I'd have been done. Finished. In the instant itself you don't look at what's right or wrong, you just do what you're going to do and that reaction just came out of me. It wasn't a preconceived line. But if I hadn't done that it would've been disastrous in my life, because Rio was still new, still sussing people out and he would never have respected me. From there, our relationship never looked back.

There were, of course, other instances of players just not taking to me at all. Ravel Morrison, a wonderfully talented but emotionally volatile young player, didn't buy into my way of working in the gym. I had issues with Michael Stewart, Mark Bosnich and David May as well. Those are the ones who stand out in my memory. Now, this is no slight whatsoever on their ability or their characters; we just didn't click as people and as a coach I wasn't able to get the maximum out of them. That is as much down to my inability to figure out how to motivate them as any aversion to gym work on their part.

Whether it worked out or not in every case, I'm thankful to every single player I interacted with, because each instance was part of my education as a coach. I learn something new every single day and those early lessons at United were absolutely invaluable for me.

A brutal one was that football moves quickly, and that getting too attached to players was a dangerous game. Jaap was one of my best friends at the club in that first couple of years. He was a colossus of a defender who could scare the life out of opponents, but he was also a softly-spoken gentleman off the pitch. Extremely funny, very dry, super pleasant. He was also a winning machine. He'd arrived at United a year before me and won the Treble in his first season, followed by Premier League titles in each of the next two campaigns. He was a champion in each of his three seasons in England. Then, suddenly, he was gone.

The first I knew of it was one Sunday morning in August

2001 when he came into the gym at Carrington, looked at me with tears in his eyes and just said: "They're selling me."

He explained to me what had happened. He'd helped to write a book over in Holland which, when translated, appeared to suggest that he'd been tapped up by United, which is to say that he'd been enticed away while still under contract at PSV Eindhoven. This created something of a stir in the English press and, a few days later, Jaap was told that United had accepted an offer from Lazio and that he'd be moving to Italy.

He was devastated and he just couldn't understand that Sir Alex Ferguson would sanction his sale.

"I can't believe he's getting rid of me because of this book," he kept saying. I couldn't believe it either. I was devastated on a personal level and confused that the best centre-back at the club was suddenly on his way out.

I heard later that the deal had nothing to do with Jaap's book. Lazio had come in with a big offer which United thought was too good to resist, especially after twice breaking the club record transfer fee for Ruud and Seba Veron earlier that summer. The gaffer actually thought Jaap had lost a little bit of his edge and sharpness, so it seemed an opportune time to get rid of a player who wouldn't have much resale value for much longer.

Within a couple of years, he'd done so well in Italy that he joined AC Milan, who knocked us out of the Champions League on their way to the final in 2005. The gaffer, to his credit, repeatedly cited Jaap's sale as one of the biggest mistakes of his career, so he certainly took a lot from the experience. As did I – don't get too attached to any player, because one day they can be working away in your gym, the next they could be having a medical at another club. Football can be a harsh business at times, as I'd be frequently reminded down the years.

CHAPTER 9

Filth

"I've had doors kicked in and walls punched through. There have been weights and fire extinguishers thrown at me more than once. Coincidentally, it was around this point that I upped my meditation."

In my first year at United, I was struck by how hard it would be for drugs to pervade football. While there had been famous cases of players taking them recreationally, I just couldn't see how a footballer would be able to improve their performance through drug-taking.

That was something I had to reflect on at the time because my past encounters with drug-takers almost culminated in Manchester United's first power development coach having his head caved in.

For context, back when I was coaching at Shapes, I started noticing that people were coming through the gym door and within six to nine months, were big, heavily built monsters, whereas I was training hard every single day and still resembled a well-defined rodent.

I was looking at training, nutrition, methodologies and watching the superstar bodybuilders, and I was thinking to myself: *I've been training hard now for 18 months, two years, why am I not developing like these guys?* It was very difficult to develop and put weight on. I'd pitch myself against most of them with regards to lifting things, being fit, strong and healthy and all the rest of it, but I was nowhere near their levels of muscle development.

There was no real form to them, it was almost like fat or water. They looked misshapen and they were out of proportion. They suddenly had square jaws, their voices were changing and they were becoming generally more aggressive around the place.

I had a big interest in nutrition and I was making packs of supplements to sell in the little family shop. We were selling proteins and supplements, but the main things that people came in and asked for were steroids. In my naivety, I hadn't realised just how prevalent it was. These people were coming in and they wanted everything in a rush. I'd spent a lot of time training to get myself in decent shape, but the results I was getting were nothing like what some of these people were achieving – however odd they looked.

I used to go to bodybuilding competitions and I hate to say it, but I actually entered into two of them. I was so skinny compared to the others that you wouldn't have believed it. I was in good shape for a layman, but next to those watery brutes I looked like I'd entered a novelty category by myself. It was an embarrassment but, looking back, it was useful because it opened my eyes. I was quite happy with how I looked, but not compared to them.

Going into those competitions I just looked ridiculous. I'm sure people would have been sniggering at the buff jockey. These goliaths with all their muscle and their aggression. To me, they had no room to be laughing at anyone. Personality is so important when you're doing anything. You can look any way you like, but if the personality doesn't fit the look then it's not authentic and that radiates. These people are very wimpish in some ways because they're so insecure. They know they've lied and cheated. They've got their huge armament, but they've not earned it and they've no idea what to really do with it, so the aggression, I always thought, was a mask for their insecurity.

You can only take steroids for so long, I believe, because then you start getting the opposite effects whereby the body starts trying to balance out the testosterone levels with oestrogen so they end up with what the community lovingly refers to as 'bitch tits'. Users go through phases of looking good, shaping up, cutting fats out to look lean as they go into a bodybuilding show, but after that they're going through a breaking down process where they're aghast at what they're looking like and they have to get back on the steroids again to build up their bodies and minds. There's so much insecurity in the process.

At the time, there was no testing in bodybuilding so, in the absence of rules, people were just doing whatever they wanted to. I was training my kids and their mates, so my gym was mainly full of youngsters. Then these lumps start coming through the door, then you see the attitudes, how they walk around, how they ringfence their space. I had to make it clear to them that this wasn't acceptable in my gym. It was always the same conversation, pretty much word-for-word, done as diplomatically as it could be.

"This isn't the place for you."

"What do you mean?"

"The type of training we do here, it's not the same as what you're doing."

"What are you trying to say?"

"Well, you're taking."

"How can you say that? Don't give me that."

"I've watched people training for years, I know what I'm talking about and you're taking drugs, as far as I'm concerned. I don't want that in my gym."

You can imagine how that went down every time. They'd kick off, swear at me, tell me I was a little skinny prick, then off they'd go and then word would start to go round among those circles. They'd often come back in a fury. I've had doors kicked in and walls punched through.

As well as abuse, there have been weights and fire extinguishers thrown at me more than once. I'd be off in the mill doing a job and someone would come and tell me that so-and-so had arrived to use the gym, and this person would be a very dangerous individual. This kind of thing went on for a while. Coincidentally, it was around this point that I upped my meditation.

There was one guy who came to the gym called Carl. He was an ex-boxer and a really nice lad, so we'd struck up a good friendship.

At one stage, I had a period off work because I was ill, so I handed the gym over to Fred, a mate of mine, to run in my absence. Fred was a big lad who'd been in prison, and by the time I came back to work, the place was full of drug-takers and the kids had virtually disappeared. As you can imagine, I upset a lot of people after that as I looked to reinstate my policies. Carl used to drop me home after training, and one night I said to him: "You can see what's going on in the gym with drugs and I'm not having it. Make me one promise: if you ever start taking drugs, you'll leave the gym." He looked at me – and this guy was a big, powerful lad, so I quickly added: "I'm not accusing you, but if you do, please, as friends, just go to one of the other gyms. You don't need to be in mine."

After a short while, Carl disappeared, which I found very sad.

* * *

Around that time, Sue and I split up, and for a year I almost rotted because I moved into the gym. A couple of friends of mine dragged me out, slapped me about a bit and said it was time for me to snap out of it and start going out again.

It's not relevant to the story in any way, but that meant I had to go clothes shopping for the first time in my life. My mum had always bought them until I got together with Sue, from which point my new wife dressed me because she hated the clothes my mum had bought me. Suddenly I was cast out into the world. After a while of living alone in the gym, my clothes had not only become less relevant to wider trends, they also had holes in them. I was technically homeless and I pretty much looked the part. My mates made it clear to me in no uncertain terms that if they were going to take me out clubbing and reintroduce me into the real world, I needed to sort out my attire. "You can't go out like that, you c***," was Frank's line.

Frank was good for morale.

The plan for that first night out was simple: they were taking me out so I could find a woman. So they took me shopping, decked me out in some ludicrous clothes, revelled in telling me how much they suited me and off we went into the night. On the way out, my thoughts were all about what I was going to say and do. I'd not entered into a romantically-motivated conversation with a woman since I was 16. I knew that I was about to be thrown in at the deep end and I'd have to learn to swim.

During the evening, we went to a nightclub in Stalybridge called Grays. As soon as I walked through the door, I could feel a funny atmosphere in the place. I went straight to the bar to order a round of drinks, and suddenly this cold feeling came over me. I thought nothing of it until, having received our drinks, I started looking around the club and realised that there were suddenly lots of big guys in our vicinity.

I said to Frank: "Does this place give you a strange feeling?"

"Very strange. I've seen some of these guys before at your gym."

Right on cue, one guy came over to me, with another three behind him.

"You're that puny little shit from Olympic, aren't you?"

"I'm from Olympic, yeah. And compared with you, I suppose I am pretty puny, yeah."

"You kicked me out of your gym, said I was on drugs."

So I looked at him.

"Well, was I right?"

Of course, that just angered him further.

"You'd better get out of here, you little prick."

That was suddenly easier said than done, as roughly 12 of his mates came from nowhere and surrounded me.

Frank was still stood by me but, because of the music, he

couldn't hear what was being said. I shouted at him to get out of there as fast as he could because things were about to kick off. I suppose he'd probably arrived at that conclusion himself, since I was suddenly pressed against the bar by a dozen giants. As they continued to berate me, he was forced out of the way anyway.

In that kind of situation, your brain tends to let you down. *Shit. I'm in bother, here. I've talked my way out of some situations in the past, but I'm out of ideas here.*

Thanks, brain. They were getting more and more aggressive. The threats weren't even vague anymore.

"We're going to take you around the back and kick the shit out of you."

Thankfully, I became aware of a commotion at the back of the crowd, the group began parting and this big guy wandered through.

It was Carl.

Carl, the ex-boxer. Carl, one of the hardest guys I'd ever met. He put his arm around my shoulder. By this time he was huge, so it was clear what he'd been up to.

"Hiya, Mick. How are ya?"

"Er, not so well at the minute."

"No, you're not. And you're probably not in the right place, are you?"

The group of lads began animatedly discussing the situation with Carl, who it turned out was the club's head bouncer, boss of most of these lads. He ushered them away and turned back to me.

"Listen, this isn't the place for you to be. Finish your drink, leave, don't look back. Don't worry about it, I'm looking after you, but don't ever come here again."

After that, we had a quick chat in which he asked about the kids. He knew that they were Olympic lifters at the world championships or playing for Manchester United, so we had a little bit of a catch-up, but I drained my drink pretty quickly and scarpered out of there as soon as I could. If Carl hadn't shown up when he did, I wouldn't be writing this book today.

Down the years, whenever I've suspected anybody I've worked with of taking any type of drug or being a total pisshead, I've told them that they shouldn't be in sport and I don't want them in my gym. Simple as that. I can't succeed as a coach for people who want their sons and daughters to become top-line sports people when you've got a drug influence in the place. Nowadays, the norm in gyms is that somebody somewhere in there will be supplying drugs. Now, we will not allow that in our family gym. Some gyms do. We will not sell drugs ourselves. You can't control what people do outside the gym in their own space, naturally, but as long as they're not doing it on your premises and you don't find them in little groups causing trouble by spreading their filth, you've done all you can.

Over the years, I've had a couple of people come into Olympic and try to spread their filth, but they didn't last long. Naturally, I'm not going to divulge those names because I don't want to be dredged out of Ashton Canal somewhere down the line.

Not all coaches have been quite so vigilant about keeping drugs out of sport, as everyone knows, and they are a major problem now. Unfortunately for my lads Mark and Shaun, as weightlifters they were involved in a sport that was heavily infected by drugs. At least in Britain they are very strict about drug testing. I had to see them both go through the rigorous testing regime which I totally understand and agree with. The only problem is, if you have those standards in Britain, then you would hope that it would be the same across the whole world, in the name of fairness, but I'm not sure how true that is. The lads were up against it. They were doing really well in Britain, but when it came to world events, they didn't know what they were up against and often it was quite clear that they weren't competing on a level playing field.

In an industry where marginal gains can make big differences and there are lots of nefarious external influences on individuals, I can understand why some give in to temptation and take drugs, but it is a terrible decision. They can be very effective in certain sports, but ultimately they affect the mentality of the person taking them, and that can be for a short time very, very positive, but ultimately very, very negative. For all the gains you get from drugs, there is a definite deficit to follow afterwards – not necessarily physically, but psychologically, mentally, emotionally. That can cause untold damage in a person's psyche.

I've worked with all kinds of athletes across most sports and I've been most impressed with football in terms of its ability to remain drug-free. It appears – and I can only commit to appears – to be the best sport at keeping drug-free. I am as absolutely certain as I can be that there was nothing like that going on at United. I spent a lot of time with every one of those players and saw no evidence of anything. Honestly, while I can see how some sports are perfectly suited to drug use, football just isn't there.

There are so many assets and facets to being a footballer. You're on one leg at virtually all times, using your feet to make art, and those feet need to be so well tuned. That's the brain sending messages right the way down to the furthest extent of the body, to be able to do things that people would normally do with their hands. Guitarists, for instance, are excellent at multi-tasking, but there's such a difference when someone's out on the pitch, moving at incredible speed, accelerating and decelerating, with so many different possibilities and so many different players on the pitch, one ball, one goal to attack, one goal to defend, referees, big crowds and so much emotion around all of this.

I doubt, personally, that drugs could be really, really effective in football. I'm not a scientist and I haven't spent time collecting evidence to prove a point either way but, in essence, I would imagine that football is the cleanest sport because of the multi-tasking of the brain, of the body, of all the different aspects required to play the game. You might get an isolated person trying it, it might be successful for a limited period of time, but that will be followed by longer periods of things going wrong. If you look at anybody who's addicted to drugs, they'll have their high points – why else would it be called getting high? – where they produce exceptional art or music or whatever, but the loss of time they'll suffer from the comedown would manifest in irregularities of being good and bad.

In football, they play so many games over a year, you've got to be playing or training almost all the time. If you look at weightlifting in comparison, if you're at a good standard then at most you'll do four competitions in the space of a year. For each of those, you're in a three-month period of building up to hit the height, then you drop off, everything disappears and then you can build up again. It lends itself to drug-taking a lot more than football, where you're in playing a game, then out recovering, on a near-constant loop. I don't see drugs as having the opportunity to infiltrate football.

Competitiveness is a wonderful thing. In my lab, I have a head-tennis court at one end of the facility. That's where the really heated debates happen, because the athletes will do anything to win. Doesn't matter if they're mates, siblings or strangers. I've seen so many instances of rule-breaking down the years because, in those situations, the tension rises and people show you just how desperate they are to win. I actually have other athletes step in and referee quite often, just so they can see the lengths that people will go to in order to achieve victory. While I love to see that kind of desire, it's absolutely vital that they stay on the right side of the line – otherwise, if they stray into cheating, then it goes against the fundamental essence of sport.

CHAPTER 10

Oh Teddy, Teddy...

"I'd have the pads on with Roy Keane and I'd just pipe up, 'Remember Teddy Sheringham? He was fantastic to train. Excellent boxer.' It used to really get Roy going."

At the start of 2000/01, my first full season working with the first team on a daily basis, I was part of a meeting with the rest of the coaching staff – the likes of assistant manager Steve McClaren, goalkeeping coach Tony Coton, first-team coach Jim Ryan, sports psychologist Bill Beswick and, naturally, Sir Alex Ferguson.

Those meetings were annual affairs involving a lot of looking to the future. During the course of this particular discussion, I was asked who the fittest player in the squad was. Who did I think was going to hit the ground running in the new campaign? Rather than chirp up with the obvious names like Keane, Beckham or Giggs, I picked the oldest outfield player in the squad: Teddy Sheringham.

To say my answer met with mirth would be an understatement. I understood why, of course, since Teddy would be 35 by the end of the season, but – as I explained to them – I was only going off what I'd seen.

From my early experiences of Teddy, I could see that he was very good in the gym, but I also wanted to go out and watch training as well. The football pitch is, after all, the players' natural environment and where they'll be showing their best and truly applying their fitness.

Traipsing out there in the training gear the club had given me, namely the same kit the players wore, didn't go down too well. I was stood watching what was going on and obviously resembled a player in Teddy's peripherals, so he shouted over: "Just fuck off out of the way, will you? Get back to the gym."

Again, your heart's in your mouth for a second because footballers don't hold back when they give you stick, especially when you've gotten in the way of the game.

In that situation, a lot of it is about sorting out your personality and deciding how strong you're going to be. I've seen people really, really collapse because of what players have said to them – people in floods of tears – but they're just finding out your personality and seeing where your boundaries are. If you can't take it, the players do adjust and calm it down because they're top-line lads.

A few minutes later, they all came back into the gym for a session. After a little while, Teddy was complaining, asking when the session was going to finish because it was going to be dark by the time we were done.

"Don't worry Teddy," I said, "I'll wander about in front of your car in a high-vis jacket waving flags so you can see what's what."

There was a bit of back-and-forth that followed, and again I was left thinking it had gone badly. I was still in my first season training adult athletes and I was increasingly convinced I wasn't doing well with Teddy. As it happened, after that session I went into the sports hall, I was boxing with Roy and Wes, and Teddy was stood on the balcony overhead, watching everything that was going on. He shouted down: "When you're finished, can I have a word with you? I want you to meet somebody." So, once I'd finished the session, he came down and walked through the door with his son.

"This is my boy, Charlie. I'd like you to coach him."

I think that's the biggest honour you can get, for a parent to say: "I want you to train my child." It's happened a few times down the years with Premier League footballers I've known. I've trained Joe van der Sar, Noah Solskjaer, Josh Ireland and Will Jaaskelainen, among others, and I've always regarded that as the greatest honour you can have as a coach because those parents are entrusting you with the development of the most important thing in their lives.

Anyway, once I'd sorted out my attire to watch training in a safer capacity, I had concluded that Teddy was the player giving off the best impression. There were players who were faster, had more endurance, more power, more strength – but it had to be everything together and it had to be football specific, and he just looked in such good shape as the season went on. It's a cliché to say that Teddy had a great 'football brain', but he was brighter in his mind than the other players, on a level with Scholesy. Every time I saw him on the pitch, he looked sharp and lively, everything just looked to be right in his world.

So, although the other coaches may have had a little snigger at my prediction, Teddy went on to have easily his best season at United. He got better and better as the campaign wore on and he ended up winning the PFA Player of the Year and FWA Player of the Year awards at the end of the season, which were nice little extras on top of his third straight Premier League winner's medal.

The gym was a huge part of Teddy's success, but I wasn't making him go in there. He was just training more because the gym was there, whereas previously there hadn't been that option. He liked being in there and, during that period, he just became the fittest player because he was training hard. A possible explanation materialised towards the end of the campaign because he was coming to the end of his contract with the club. He really wanted to stay at United and was hoping for a two-year extension, but they only offered him one. I spent a lot of time with Teddy, and he was so disappointed with the club's one-year offer. We used to chat, we talked about where he was going to go, what he was going to do and he ended up leaving at the end of the season to rejoin Tottenham.

The other coaches regularly brought up my pre-season prediction during the course of the campaign, especially when Teddy starting picking up the major individual awards, and I think I have a lot to thank him for, because as much as my early work was winning over the players, I also had to prove that I knew what I was talking about in the meeting rooms.

After a relatively frosty start, we got on really well and I did miss having him around the place. Teddy was a very bright guy with a sharp wit, so he was good company to have in the gym. But his departure didn't mean that I wasn't able to use his memory around Carrington.

You see, he and Roy weren't the best friends. Roy just outright didn't like him. I think Teddy was maybe a bit too flamboyant for him. A smart, good-looking guy with a lot of confidence, so I don't know if that maybe wound Roy up. It wouldn't take much for two players to not get on. They didn't have to be best friends to win trophies together. There was certainly something there between them so, even after he'd gone, I used to use Teddy as a way of winding Roy up. I'd have the pads on and I'd just pipe up: "Remember Teddy? He was fantastic to train. Excellent boxer."

It used to really get Roy going. I found his weakness in that, and I'd exploit it to get him really wound up. It was my way of prodding him, motivating him. It was a stimulant to maximise his performance. Had he lamped me, I could have protested that I was just doing my job!

CHAPTER 11

The Right Side

"Even in that squad of hugely dedicated athletes, nobody came close to David Beckham at the bleep test. He was incredible to watch; so far ahead of everybody else that it was ridiculous."

One lesson which I quickly learnt in my first year or two at United was how badly misjudged the players were by the outside world.

Don't get me wrong; initially it was a faintly surreal experience for a lifelong fan like myself to be suddenly plunged into an environment where I was working with some of the most famous sportsmen in the world, but it didn't take me long to realise just how normal these people really were.

Put it this way: if I hadn't already known who they were, how much they'd won and how much they earned, it could easily have been a bunch of lads just like I had seen time and time again during my years at Olympic. The players at United were characterised as these rich egomaniacs who were there to be shot at, but they were just normal blokes with normal lives, save for their extraordinary talent.

It began to really bother me how much nonsense they had to put up with when, for the vast majority of the time, everything else was just background noise behind the football. In September 2000, David Beckham walked into the gym and within seconds the radio, which we always had on, started blaring out the news. One of their headline stories was that David was in the midst of suing Walkers because they had announced plans to launch a new flavour of crisp called Smokey Beckham. The lads were all pissing themselves, not least David, who had absolutely no idea about the whole ordeal. It was totally fabricated. That opened my eyes. As funny as that was at the time, it was also pitiful in a sense because suddenly David had to defend himself, despite being the victim.

These days David is, of course, a megastar who has transcended football completely. He has to be one of the most recognisable figures in the world, and he was certainly well on his way to fame by the time I took the job at United. He was a brilliant footballer, of course, but his commitment to excellence was what made him so good. He was so fit, so energetic, so mindful of the team's fortunes, that he was able to provide incredible defensive support to Gary Neville while still doing a brilliant job going forward on the right wing. Goals, assists, tracking back; he was a model professional, and my word, did he put in the hard yards.

Bleep tests were a fairly well-known part of a footballer's training regime at the time. The basic premise is to run back and forth between two markers before a machine emits a loud bleep. The time between bleeps shortens, forcing the individual to run faster in order to keep up with them. Even in that squad of hugely dedicated athletes, nobody came close to David Beckham. He was incredible to watch; so far ahead of everybody else that it was ridiculous.

I think he was quite an obsessive character in general when it came to preparation. I remember when our Michael was coming up through the ranks at United at 16, he would go to the Cliff to train two or three days a week, and every time he went, Beckham was there too. He'd done his own training already that day, but was doing extra sessions with the kids as well.

On a personal level, I found him to be an absolute gentleman who always had time for people and was never afraid of asking questions. By the time I first came into contact with him, he already had a couple of tattoos. He was desperate for more though, and he'd clearly developed a taste for them.

At the time, during what would prove to be his penultimate season at the club, we had a series of chats about it and we actually ended up sketching a few potential designs together. I can't draw, but it was all about trialling different ideas, so we just sat there at my desk in the gym, scribbling away. It culminated in the number seven in Roman Numerals on his forearm. Now, seven has a relevance to God, with 777 being God's perfect number, and we talked a lot about that. That perfection in God's number was the same as the perfection David was chasing as a player, so in many ways it was perfect that he wore that shirt at United.

That obsessive behaviour which underscored Beckham's training was evident in all those boys: Gary Neville, Phil Neville, Scholesy, Butty. When David was doing extra work with the younger age group, all those lads were involved too. Gary gained himself a reputation as a character who loved to moan, but that was just the manifestation of his relentless drive. He was totally focused on carving out a career at the club he loved, and it meant so much to him that he wanted everything in his preparation to be perfect, from nutrition to tactics.

One of the most high-level conversations I ever heard about football was between Gary and Carlos Queiroz, discussing the role of United's right-back after David Beckham had left and Cristiano Ronaldo had come in. They both spoke passionately about it, put their cases forward with really sound arguments and it was fascinating to listen to. It struck me how much Gary understood and cared about his job.

While Gary was always compelled to share his opinions, I always found him incredibly easy to deal with when it came to the gym. He would do whatever he was told to and never said much except to ask what he should do next. He never batted an eyelid when I was telling him what needed to be done, and we had a really strong working relationship – one which stepped up a level around the same time I had helped David with his tattoo designs. Gary had started having lessons with a guitar tutor, but the story leaked into the press and his tutor then dramatically inflated the price of lessons as a result. Obviously Gary could have afforded it, but being such a principled individual, he refused flat out. Quite right, too.

Now, in a previous conversation, I had made Gary aware of my days on the Yorkshire music circuit. I had played bass, but I knew a few basics of playing a standard guitar. He told me about his issue with the tutor and that he now expected any tutor to charge him an unfair fee, so I offered to show him a few bits and bobs to get him started. Sure enough, he brought his guitar to Carrington a few days later and over the next few weeks we had maybe 10 or 15 basic guitar lessons in the gym after the first-team session had finished and before the young lads came in to do their afternoon work. We had a great time. I wasn't a very good guitarist at all – shite, to be honest with you – but I knew a little bit more about it than the person I was teaching, and that was enough to make a little bit of progress. I never would have charged Gary for it, of course, but once he'd progressed as far as I could take him, he gave me an acoustic guitar, which I still cherish as a lovely memento.

Over the years, football has changed beyond recognition in terms of finance and fame. Later in my career, post-United, I had the opportunity to work with an awful lot of young professional footballers from various clubs, mainly based in the north-west. They'd come into my lab in Ashton and do their work, but a lot of the time they'd be chatting amongst themselves about going to the Trafford Centre later that night, where they'd be thrilled by the prospect of being recognised. They wanted the buzz of being asked for their autograph. It was almost a plague, this obsession that they all had with fame, with having the right hair, the right clothes, the little bag, the right car. It was all back to front. They were fixated on having all accessories rather than the core. When I asked them about their sleep patterns and diets, they couldn't give me any information. They just shrugged. Those were the details that mattered to the best of the best.

When I first started out at United, it always struck me that despite the enormous, unfathomable amount of attention trained on the sport and the players in particular, at their core they were totally run-of-the-mill people, no different to you or I. The difference between the also-rans and the greatest ever was their focus on the right facets of their lives. Everything was in perfect working order and that was how they were able to reach such levels of stardom.

CHAPTER 12

Michael

*"If I could go back over my entire coaching
career again and train just one athlete differently,
it would be Michael. My work for United,
with those star players, overshadowed the work
I should have been doing with my own son."*

Everybody has regrets in their life and I'm no different. One of my biggest involves our Michael.

My eldest son being a United player was one of my greatest sources of pride. I loved knowing that he played for one of the biggest football clubs in the world, loved watching him play at Old Trafford and loved seeing the joy that brought him. His dream had come true. I suppose, on a personal level, as well as the paternal pride, I was proud that despite not being the most naturally gifted player, Michael had made it through the hard graft and physical prowess I'd drilled into all of the kids from an early age.

Then, when I started working at United, it became one of my biggest problems.

I had to spend so much time with first-team players on a personal basis. Whatever they wanted from the gym, I was to provide for them, and I'd like to think I did that. I gave each player as much time as I could because it was my job to try to improve them all for first-team duty. At that time, Michael was very often doing reserve team training, which limited my contact with him and I found that difficult.

Michael made his first-team debut in 1996, nearly four years before I arrived at the club. He made six appearances that season, all-told, but of course he was competing for a place with Gary Neville. Whenever he got a chance, he did well, but the gaffer had decided that Gary was his first choice and that was fair enough. Gary rarely missed games, he was a great professional, a great defender, and also he had a phenomenal partnership down the right-hand side with David Beckham, so Michael didn't have much of a chance to stake a claim. He was essentially competing with a partnership which had established itself for United and England.

By the end of the Treble season, shortly before I joined, Michael had made 16 appearances for the first team. He only made another eight over the next three seasons after I arrived. He was trying and trying to get back into the first team, he was made captain of the Reserves, but from Sir Alex Ferguson's point of view, that wasn't a role that he wanted a player to have for too long because it meant they were stagnating. Michael had it for quite a while, then lost it to Michael Stewart, the young Scottish midfielder who the manager was trying to encourage, and it was really heart-breaking to see my lad's dream slowly dying.

If I could go back over my entire coaching career again and train just one athlete differently, it would be Michael. Definitely. I put all the emphasis of his training on power, physicality and athleticism. I didn't focus enough on specificity to football. In some ways, the way I approached coaching him was akin to modern day sports science, because I made him particularly adept at deadlifts, squats, running between two poles and so on, but I didn't put enough specific footballing techniques into his work.

If I'd thought more in terms of football skill as well as speed and strength, I think he would have been a lot more successful. The specific skills for the sport have to be loaded in with the speed, strength, power, cognition and multi-tasking. That's what I've got now and why I'm really happy with how I train athletes now. I would use my current set-up as a training model anywhere for any sport.

I wanted to help him more. Absolutely. We did extra work together. We did various things together, but we didn't have the time to really look at him as an individual and devote ourselves to improving him, which is one of the saddest points of my career. And of my life, I suppose. My work for United, with those star players, overshadowed the work I should have been doing with my own son. And that's one of the commitments I had to stick to. That was a hard, hard one, for him and for me, and before long Michael had drifted into a position where he knew he had to move on.

Of course, I knew this too, but it still didn't make it any easier when I had the situation quite emphatically confirmed to me ahead of the 2001/02 season. There was a meeting between the coaching staff where the squad was assessed and both incomings and outgoings were discussed. The gaffer, Steve McClaren, Mike Phelan, myself and Bill Beswick made up the discussion.

These were a fairly regular occurrence. Sir Alex used to let these meetings go on and didn't really say much. He'd let it go and only intervene if it was necessary and generally let us sort things out ourselves. That's how he ran things, to get the best out of his staff: he gave them power to do things and decide things, only intervening if required. In this particular case, everyone talked about transfer targets – huge sums were being spent on Juan Sebastian Veron and Ruud van Nistelrooy – and then the conversation moved on to who was going to make room for the newcomers.

The group listed a few fringe players and then Bill said: "Cleggy is one who has to go."

There aren't the words to describe that moment in your life. Everything freezes.

Even though I knew it was coming at some point, it was one of the biggest shocks of my life.

But I couldn't flinch. I couldn't show them any emotion.

That moment reminded me of the day of Michael's trial.

That day, when he was 15, he'd played in his trial match for United and he'd been sensational. He was everywhere on the pitch, passing, tackling, sprinting about like a madman. He was omnipresent.

Afterwards, United's Under-16s manager, Dave Bushell, was talking to the team about the game. He purposely went through all the goalscorers and missed out Michael's name. He looked around and asked the room: "Who got the other goal? Who else scored?"

As a parent, you're screaming inside.

IT WAS OUR MICHAEL. MICHAEL CLEGG.

Dave looked at me, waiting to see if I'd jump in. He looked at Michael, waiting to see if he'd put his hand up and take the acclaim.

Neither of us flinched.

That was the day the dream began. Eight years later, I didn't flinch on the day the dream was over. Possibly the rest of the coaching staff would have been ready for a reaction from me. Maybe it was even done the way it was so that they could see what kind of person I was. Maybe they wanted to know if I could cope with the difficult aspects that can arise in football. It happens, you know. Fergie had to sell his own son, Darren, early in his time at United. It's an unpleasant, awful part of the job but sometimes it pans out that way.

It's interesting that Bill was the one to deliver the news, but in his professional capacity he was paid to judge who was giving the most psychologically and who wasn't, and when he looked around at the different players, maybe Michael wasn't giving enough compared to the others. I can see it from a psychological role.

After the meeting, Bill pulled me to one side.

"Mick, that must have been really, really hard for you."

It was, of course, but I just repressed the reality of my emotion at the time. You're paid to do a job and at the end of the day I was. My main job was first-team players playing on a regular basis. My son wasn't among those players.

Michael had to go in and see the gaffer soon afterwards, and he had the news confirmed to him.

We never spoke about it. We didn't have to. We were both gutted. Michael and I had been at United together for a couple of years, but now it was over.

United was all he'd ever known. He'd not been signed by any other club when he was younger. Never had a trial for a professional team before his trial with United, and after that he'd gone straight in after three months and never looked back. He'd played in all sorts of games, including a Champions League quarter-final against Monaco, then suddenly he was

23 years old, the wow factor around him had gone and he had been told that he was on his way. Naturally, he was absolutely demolished.

I went back to Brian Poole, who had first spotted him all those years ago. I noticed that Iain Dowie, who was then Oldham's assistant manager, was watching a United Reserves game at Altrincham, and Michael had an absolute blinder. Brian still had strong links to Oldham, so I told him that United were letting Michael go, and that I knew Iain had just seen him do really well for the Reserves. Brian had a word and Oldham signed him up straight away on a three-year contract. I was thrilled. Michael went straight out and it became a case of rooting for him to do well with a fresh start. He really wanted to do well for Oldham but, for whatever reason, it just didn't work out for him. I think over a period of time, he just stopped enjoying football. The first eight or 10 weeks went well; he was playing and performing, but the manager, Mick Wadsworth, was sacked less than four months after Michael joined. Dowie stepped up to replace him as manager and played Michael in his first few games but then Iain started looking elsewhere as he built the team how he wanted it to be.

Michael just continued to fall out of love with the game and he ended up retiring at 27.

I have no issue at all with anybody over how things went. I had no problem with the gaffer over it, and we got on famously for the best part of a decade after that. Likewise, I had no issue with Bill as the bearer of bad news. I kept working with him and even long after he left United, I spoke alongside him at an event in Manchester where we were both discussing Guillem Balague's book about Cristiano Ronaldo, and it was fantastic to catch up with him. Honestly, I recognise that it was business, he was doing his job and I bear nobody any ill will whatsoever. My only regret is how I acted, that I didn't do more to help my lad.

It's funny, though: you never know what will happen next in life. Michael had grown up around me coaching various athletes and I'd given him quite a few opportunities to help me out with coaching down the years, so he picked up more and more of the art of coaching as time passed by. After he retired from football, he came back to Olympic, did a lot more work with me and developed into a really top-level power development coach.

When Roy Keane stepped into management for the first time, taking on the Sunderland job in 2006, he sounded me out to see if I would be interested in joining him at the Stadium of Light as part of the coaching team. When it became clear that I wouldn't leave United, he asked me if I thought that Michael would be able to do the job.

"Of course he could," I said. "Without a doubt."

Roy was made up with this. He knew Michael's character already, having worked with him during his eight years at the club, plus he knew – like all the players did – how physically adept Michael was, so he was prepared to take a punt on him.

There's a strange symmetry about how things went. My career at United really took off because of the work I did with Roy Keane, then he ended up giving my son his chance in coaching. Michael ended up spending a dozen years at Sunderland, becoming one of the outstanding power development coaches around, renowned across the industry. His journey ended up going full circle when Ole Gunnar Solskjaer became United manager permanently in 2019. Ole quickly identified the need for his squad to become fitter and stronger. He sat next to Michael in the first-team dressing room during their time together as players, so he knew all about his character, knew that he'd established himself as one of the best coaches in the industry and, most importantly, he knew he was available after leaving Sunderland. So, ahead of the 2019/20 season, Michael accepted an offer from Ole to return to United as the lead power development coach, working on a daily basis in the same gym I'd run 20 years earlier. Life has a funny way about it.

So, while I do still have regrets about not doing more to help Michael with his playing career, I honestly couldn't be any prouder of him and the career he's carved for himself.

CHAPTER 13

The Unconscious Mind

"One of the hardest things in sport – in life, even – is to follow through and do what you say you're going to do, but Ruud did it that day and it was absolutely magnificent to watch."

One of the most influential figures I came across in my career was Ruud van Nistelrooy. Working with him actually sewed seeds which would sprout an entirely new way of thinking for me, albeit years after we'd finished working together.

When Ruud first came over to Manchester from PSV Eindhoven in 2001, he was returning from anterior cruciate ligament damage and actually arrived a year after he was initially scheduled to join United. He was very intelligent, a real thinker and he knew all about the surgery he'd had, down to the finer details. He'd kept copies of all his medical notes from his rehabilitation and he told me all the stories of what he did, how he felt physically every step of the way, and we pieced together a very detailed routine for all aspects of his training. He became very successful and scored a lot of goals for United. He was in a great team, of course, so that definitely helped him because of the number of chances served up by players like Beckham, Giggs and so on, but what a superb, instinctive player he was. Ruud taught me a number of lessons, one being the importance of being able to back up what you say.

About 18 months after he'd joined, we were talking in the gym and the conversation turned to 'boxes', a training drill whereby two players are boxed in by seven or eight team-mates and their job is to intercept and retrieve the ball while it's being passed among the other players. When this happens, the player whose pass was intercepted then trades places with the player in the middle and then they have to chase the ball. Ruud was telling me that he loved boxes, but he never went in the middle. Gary Neville, who was stood nearby, overheard the conversation and said Ruud was talking rubbish, and that the Dutchman was always in the middle.

As you would imagine, the conversation went back and forth, with both lads absolutely adamant that they were right, and I said the best way to settle it was for me to come and watch the following morning's boxes session.

So I went out there, onto the hallowed turf of the training pitch, which was set right in front of the gaffer's office. He was up there, observing as ever, and noticed me loitering. I didn't too often go out onto the training pitch and I very rarely caught the early session because there were always players that needed specialist attention in the gym. Next thing I knew, Sir Alex had put his coat on and sidled up next to me to see what was happening, giving me the usual light-hearted pleasantries like, "Get back in your cage," but I just smiled, didn't say a word and watched from afar for 20 minutes. It was obvious that some of the lads knew about the discussion between Nev and Ruud because the atmosphere was tense and the football was electric as the ball fizzed around the boxes that morning.

Guess what.

Ruud van Nistelrooy didn't once go in the centre.

Not once.

He was unbelievable. His movement and his ability were such high class; his ability to manipulate his body in all sorts of positions so that he didn't lose possession was astonishing. It was absolutely unbelievable. That's not to say he never went in the middle in his career before or after that day, because I'm sure he would have, but on the evidence I saw, he absolutely backed up his assertion. One of the hardest things in sport – in life, even – is to follow through and do what you say you're going to do, but Ruud did it that day and it was absolutely magnificent to watch.

Everything he did was so instinctive, and that tied in with a conversation I'd had with him around a year earlier, not too long after he'd joined. In spite of being out for so long with his knee injury, Ruud had started off his United career in sensational form. He was scoring for fun, and I found it so interesting to see him go from being a seriously injured player to a very, very good player who almost couldn't help but score.

So I asked him what was going on. Why was he scoring so much and always from inside the 18-yard box? That led to a fascinating conversation which has always stayed with me. Ruud said it was very important for him to understand what was happening to him, so that he could actually allow it to happen. He said that when the ball would come into the box towards him, at that moment in time when he saw the ball coming in, he would lose consciousness. He didn't mean in the sense that he went limp and collapsed, but that he lost consciousness in his head.

He went into subconscious mode. He would see the ball on its way towards him, but then he couldn't remember anything until the end, when the ball was either in the net, row Z or in the keeper's hands. More often than not, it would be in the net.

"I just do what happens and I have no control of it," he said.

That's really important to me. He lost the conscious perception of what was regularly on his mind; his awareness of field, stadium, game, opponents, position, score, time. His thoughts narrowed down to, for instance, speed of the ball approaching, speed of his movement towards the ball, searching for the ideal target to place the ball on contact to score a goal, plus recognising other defenders around him in their space and time, to avoid being blocked from placing the ball at the speed and direction needed to score.

He, from a subconscious mode, had to manoeuvre his body into the right position, use the right angles of movement to strike the ball in the required place to achieve the outcome, exercising restraint and harnessing the power of his body to exact requirements.

In order to do all this, Ruud had to leave behind normal conscious thoughts that were running around his mind and slip into a new level of consciousness to make the exact and difficult task to ensure the right outcome when attempting to score the goal.

This isn't something that just happened overnight. Ruud repeatedly practised the necessary movement under a no-pressure training situation to be honed and developed to work into the most pressurised place and time: the big match. He honed it and honed it until he could basically score goals at an almost unconscious level. When people talk about the best strikers, I've heard the throwaway comments about natural finishers who could score in their sleep. This was basically true of Ruud: he was able to score goals instinctively. He would actually score in a game without having an image of it in his mind, go to bed that night and fall asleep straight away, but then wake up a few hours later with the memory vivid in his mind.

I found that concept so compelling and it stuck with me. It was only years later that the significance of what I'd seen really became clear. I'd long since thought it was vital to train the brain over the body, because the brain controls the body. But I learned, by observing, that there was much more to it than that.

As a coach, one of the key questions is: what is the most important thing to develop in order to develop everything? By experiencing thousands of training sessions and tests, it became clear that good hand-eye coordination and foot-eye coordination are vital, and as such we're always looking to get the athlete's vision up to its most efficient aspect. Vision is the key to unlocking the brain.

Over time you realise how to harness what you've been seeing; the blending of these signals through the eyes, going through to the athletes' brain, through this consciousness. Because so many things are being done at the same time – multitasking – and being done together, you can slip from strength to speed to agility to power to skill to vision and decision-making.

Ruud, for example, had times where he would be on the

cusp of operating unconsciously in front of goal, but out of nowhere he would make a pass instead of a shot. So he's almost unconscious, and suddenly he flicks a switch in his brain and makes a pass instead. If you think in terms of boxing, you may be throwing punches and suddenly take evasive action because your opponent is throwing punches at you. In that split second you decide to change. To be able to make those decisions so quickly, you need to do something unique.

But it's not just about the brain and vision. We've also got to tap into emotion. When Aaron Cook, then the world number one taekwondo fighter, first began working with me, he was a fantastic taekwondo practitioner, but a bit wimpish, almost, as a character. He's a tremendously nice guy and he was lacking what most would call that killer instinct. If you imagine what it takes to drive your foot into somebody's neck and smash them out, you realise that we're not talking just physicality here; we're talking about emotional power.

For me, it's about understanding that the brain is important to controlling all the mechanisms, but then it's about understanding that without the vision you've got nothing; without the emotion of what is required, what is needed, then you haven't got the full story. Then it's about training in a way of manipulating all these different facets together to give you the whole picture. It's the simultaneous manipulation of brain, vision and emotion.

This led to a new kind of training for me: Quantum Consciousness Training or, as I usually refer to it, Splice Training.

You start the process of pulling in one exercise with another, knitting them together and this is quantum consciousness: the ability to fix things together so they work simultaneously and extract the maximum power from the brain. If we want to make athletes better at, for example, football, you can work on all the required facets individually to do that. It can work to a degree, but there's a better way through splicing them together. The more we do this during training, the more sports specificity we achieve.

So we start training athletes with some part strength, some part speed, some part power, some part of balance, endurance capacity, skills, but it's all guided by vision. Without the vision to see the field, then it's hopeless.

I've never heard other coaches discussing this kind of approach, which I like to think makes my style quite unique in the industry. For that, I owe an awful lot to Ruud van Nistelrooy.

CHAPTER 14

Up For The World Cup?

*"I spent the summer of 2002 on holiday in
Bognor Regis instead of Japan. Looking back,
I suppose Roy could have joined me."*

In football, the top players always have to make allowances
for international fixtures when it comes to planning their
holidays. They look at where they could be playing for their
country after the club season ends and, in the years when
there's a major summer tournament like the World Cup,
Euros, Copa America and so on, they have to factor in their
potential involvement before committing to time away with
their partner or family.

Just after Christmas in 2001, Roy came over to me in the
gym after training and asked: "What are you doing for a break
at the end of the season?"

"I'm not really sure. Haven't thought about it."

"I might have a job for you, so keep that in mind before
booking anywhere."

That's all he said. Roy being Roy, he gave me that tantalising
morsel and off he went. He was very deep at times, Roy. The

way he was reminded me of Eddie, an ex-marine who had taken me on as an apprentice at the power station. We used to play cards with the lads on shift work. Eddie taught me how to play an old card game called Don. I was 17 or 18 and Eddie hated losing. If I played the wrong card and we lost, Eddie had ways of making you realise that responsibility on shift is crucial. If I made a mistake, I knew that I would be putting shit to the shovel, rather than wiring motors at the end of the job.

With this in mind, when Roy was around, I realised that listening is two-thirds more important than talking. We have two ears and only one mouth, after all. So, even though I was naturally very curious as to what he was talking about, I just left him to it and tried not to let my mind wander too much.

A couple of weeks later he came back to me and asked me if I would like to go to the World Cup in Japan and train the Republic of Ireland national team in the same capacity as my United work. The Irish lads, he assured me, would love the boxing and speed reaction work, plus he wanted to be at his very peak for this World Cup. Roy was 30 at the time and Ireland were by no means guaranteed to qualify for each tournament, so there was a very real chance that the 2002 World Cup might be his last.

He wanted to leave no stone unturned in the pursuit of getting to that tournament at his best. Even though Ireland were nowhere near favourites for the competition, Roy would have wanted to go to Japan and win the World Cup – no doubt about it in my mind. He wasn't one who was happy to go along and make up the numbers.

To say I was chuffed would be an understatement. Inside, I felt a huge sense of worth. Using everything I'd learned over the years, I'd be given the opportunity to put it to use on the world stage. At the World Cup. That was an amazing opportunity for someone midway through just their second season in coaching at a football club.

The only caveat, Roy said, was that he first had to run it by the Ireland manager, Mick McCarthy.

Time passed and, as the tournament approached, Roy came in to see me before training one morning.

"Look, Mick, I'm really sorry about this, but me and McCarthy have had a disagreement about who should be going to the tournament. McCarthy says he doesn't know you, and he doesn't want people who he doesn't know to be part of the team."

It was quite evident from Roy's demeanour that it had been a tense discussion. McCarthy had pulled rank and refused to listen to the advantages that I could bring to the squad. He turned Roy's request down and that was the end of my World Cup involvement.

Bear in mind that Roy was in his ninth season at United at that stage, so he was used to Sir Alex Ferguson's style of management, which was ground-breaking. He had an iron grip on staff and players working to protocol that he had implemented, but he was also so open-minded to new ideas on lifestyle and training methodology. He was a big believer in marginal gains and if somebody could bring something new to the team which would make a fraction of a percent's improvement, then he was totally open to it.

Think back to my own arrival at the club. Before I was even admitted onto the coaching staff, Brian Kidd asked me about plyometrics when it was very new and football hadn't even touched it. When I did come in later on, it was at the behest of Rob Swire, who took it upon himself to think outside the box when bringing in someone to work at the Carrington gym. At that time, everywhere I looked in the backroom staff, there was evidence of Ferguson's open-minded management style. Those who he brought in were encouraged to push parameters and think differently.

Alex brought in a vision specialist to help, Gail Stephenson, who tragically is no longer with us. The difference Gail made to so many of those players can't be overstated. The same goes for the nutritionist, Trevor Lea. Trevor had a massive impact on the players, with his knowledge of dietary needs and the impact of specific nutrients, but moreover his way to translate that into food which, while fundamentally highly beneficial, was just purely enjoyable food in its own right.

Alex was known for having progressive thinkers alongside him in the dugout – Steve McClaren was a cutting-edge coach, Carlos Queiroz approached tactics in a different way to others in the business, Rene Meulensteen developed the individual skills of youth team players, then senior players, then the whole squad. These are household names now but I could list a stack of names which would be unfamiliar to virtually everyone outside of Carrington, but the contribution they made to such a successful period was massive.

Among them was psychologist Bill Beswick, who was brought in by Steve McClaren. Bill was utterly brilliant at what he did, and one aspect of his approach echoed the way that Sir Alex was able to delegate aspects of his role so well. Bill had a good way of always applauding any staff members for helping players with all sorts of personal problems and anxieties. He made staff feel great for the small emotional fixes they provided for the players. While a member of the maintenance staff or cleaning staff might seem to be worlds apart from these young multi-millionaires, they make an enormous contribution. An awful lot of them have experience of raising their own children, so they have well-developed abilities to provide guidance in various forms, and the players were very receptive to that. There was very little demarcation around Carrington because the interactions between all individuals at all levels of the club were key to a happy, healthy environment. Bill recognised that as a psychologist at the top of his field, so he did all he could to encourage it with positive feedback for the staff.

Of course, much was always made of Sir Alex being a master of mind games and being a keen psychologist himself. One day, when I had mentioned Bill to him, Ferguson said to me: "There's only one psychologist in this place, and that's me." He wasn't demeaning Bill's work, or anybody else's, he was just saying that he was the main guy. Yes, all go off and do your jobs, but remember who's ultimately in charge.

The backroom team functioned together smoothly. If a player was with me and I felt they needed some guidance on nutrition, I'd encourage them to go and see Trevor so that they had the right advice to underpin the work I was doing with them. If I sensed that something wasn't right with somebody and they had the weight of the world on their shoulders, I'd encourage them to go and see Bill. Roy was one of the first to go up and see Bill, based on me vouching for what a good guy he was.

So Roy was firmly ensconced in a culture of open-mindedness and mutual trust in the pursuit of constant improvement, and he had gone to McCarthy with the intention of introducing me to Ireland's backroom staff because he thought I would give them a better chance of winning the World Cup. When he got the knockback on that request, he was annoyed by the fixed-minded approach that he had met. He always wanted to learn and wanted others around him to want the same. If that approach was good enough for Sir Alex Ferguson, it was good enough for Mick McCarthy, he reasoned.

Obviously, I was absolutely gutted that I wouldn't be going to Japan and Roy was quite embarrassed at having to retract his offer. It was quite surreal, having had that flicker of insight into the mentality of the camp, to then see what happened when Ireland flew out to the tournament. I heard afterwards, from a lot of different sources, that the trip turned out to be very badly organised in a host of different ways, from hotels and travel to training pitches and food provisions.

That really inflamed Roy and there were always going to be ramifications from such obvious organisational problems spilling out onto the playing field, so it was no huge surprise when the news broke that there had been a very public spat between Roy and McCarthy, culminating in Roy's decision to leave the tournament.

It was a shame to see his last World Cup disappear so late in the day, but Roy Keane was a stone-cold winner who wanted the best level of preparation so that he and his team-mates had the best chance of performing well for their country. When the opposite was delivered, he just couldn't process it and felt that he had to walk away.

As for me, I spent the summer of 2002 on holiday in Bognor Regis. Looking back, I suppose Roy could have joined me. Nevertheless, he was soon on to the gaffer about taking me away on the club's pre-season tour of America, which happened ahead of the 2003/04 campaign. Now that was pressure.

I'd grown accustomed to working in Carrington, nice and enclosed, away from the prying eyes of the public. Just me, the players and maybe the odd coach now and then. Our first training session at Nike HQ in Portland took place in front of the world's media. There were TV cameras, reporters, photographers and all kinds of entourages milling about.

There were around 24 players on the tour. I set up a series of circuits, some with weights, some without, and arranged them in a circle. I had to be at the centre of the circle, so the epicentral exercise in the circuit was boxing with me. That way everybody, as they were doing their shoulder presses, squats, deadlifts and other exercises, was pointed at the boxing in the centre.

That was the central theme, so that every second of every round that was going on, everybody was looking at me. Well, not so much me as looking at the pads, looking at who was throwing the punches and judging their team-mates. Player A might have been doing bicep curls and thinking about how big their arms are, but during the circuit they were looking at Player B's fists pounding into the pads. They could judge each other.

Of course, the subplot for me, on my first tour, was that I had to show all those players that I could handle whatever they could throw at me. Each player did three rounds with me during the circuit, and each round lasted 30 seconds, short enough for every player to put everything they had into their punches. To anybody on the sidelines scanning around the scene, they must have spotted me, surrounded by goalkeepers and centre-backs, and thought to themselves: *Look at the little diddy man. He's an idiot. He's going to get killed!* Over the course of 72 rounds, I had to be able to take every one of those punches and respond well, guiding the players properly with my pads. I'd trained hard over the years and while I was no bodybuilder, I was pretty fit. But this was fitness on a far superior level to anything I'd ever done before – it wasn't about my body, it was about my mind.

I slept well that night.

Thankfully, the fitness work we did on tour was seen as a success and I was invited back on future trips. I went all over the world. In 2007, I even got to go to Japan!

CHAPTER 15

The Gaffer

"From 2003 onwards, I ended up training Sir Alex on a regular basis. As a combative character, he was another who deeply enjoyed the boxing work. As a proud and competitive Scotsman, he was also very easy to wind up."

Before I worked with Sir Alex Ferguson, the first time I ever met him was the day our Steven signed for United.

That, in itself, was an unforeseen turn of events because Steven hardly ever played football. He was brilliant at basketball and all kinds of athletic events, but he didn't really have the same enthusiasm for football. Nevertheless, he would sometimes play when asked and, because of his incredible athleticism, he always caught the eye. That was the case when he made one of his occasional outings for Tameside Boys on an afternoon when a scout from Blackburn Rovers happened to be watching.

The scout was already aware of Michael and had wanted to take him to Blackburn, so he was very excited to essentially have a free run at Steven. Blackburn sent us tickets for an upcoming game, treated us to a nice meal in a top local restaurant beforehand and then afterwards showed us around the dressing room. Maybe it was the sight of Colin Hendry's balls slapping around – an image I doubt I'll ever shake – but something told me not to sign there and then when Blackburn offered Steven a contract. The next day, I got in touch with Brian Poole, the United scout who had taken Michael in, and explained where things were at.

"I'll be back in touch with you," he said.

A few hours later, he rang back.

"I'll come pick you up on Tuesday and take you into the office to meet Alex. He wants to speak to you and Steven."

When Tuesday came, I sent Steven out to see his mates and went alone.

"I think the boss wanted to see Steven," Brian warned me.

"Well, he'll have to see me."

I'd heard about how convincing Ferguson could be. I wanted Steven to have a clear head when it came to deciding his next move, so that he did the right thing for his future. If he'd sat down in that office, his mind would have been made up before anyone had said a word. Even if Blackburn's offer – both financially and developmentally – had been better, he'd have signed with United simply because Alex Ferguson was there. It's well known that he's very good with kids; he talks to them, gives them a lot, gives them that impetus to want to work hard and train hard just because of his energy levels. He knows what to say, when and how to say it.

Needless to say, Ferguson wasn't happy when I told him that Steven was out with his mates, but we had a good chat about his prospects and there and then he promised that as soon as he finished his two years as a schoolboy, Steven would have a three-year contract with United, which was absolutely amazing for us as a family. He was assured of a five-year deal, which was unprecedented at the time.

I went away, talked things through with Steven and we went back to Ferguson's office a few days later to sign the contract and take a few pictures. After that, I didn't see the manager again for a long while, even after I'd joined the club myself.

That long-awaited third meeting took place in the canteen at Carrington a few months after I'd been on board.

He came over and was really welcoming and pleasant. "How are you? Nice to see you're working here in the gym," he said.

Me being me, I smiled and said: "Thanks. Although I haven't seen you in there yet."

"No, no, it's not for me," he laughed.

"You have to look after yourself. You're under a lot of pressure and you ought to come and see me in the gym sometime."

We left it there and he didn't come into the gym for a couple of years. He didn't listen to my advice at that stage, but his stance changed after a conversation with Roy Keane in 2003 about me going on the pre-season tour of the United States.

Following Roy's request, the boss collared me and said: "The players have been asking for you to go, would you be happy to?" Once I agreed to that, he added: "What I want you to do, while we're out there, is make sure all the staff train. You have my authority to say that to all the staff, and you're going to train me too."

So, from the summer of 2003 onwards, I ended up training Sir Alex on a regular basis. As a combative character, he was another who deeply enjoyed the boxing work. As a proud and competitive Scotsman, he was also very easy to wind up.

I'd put the pads on and set to work. I'd tell him he'd never be as good as Roy Keane, which usually met with the riposte, "Come here, you little English bastard, I'll thump you," and it was always enjoyable jousting. I'd refer to his Scottishness all the time too. He liked walking, so I'd set him off on the treadmill, crank up the incline and tell him to imagine he was marching through the Highlands in his kilt in the fresh air. It probably sounds like two old gits trading gentle xenophobia, but it was all light-hearted and he was highly enjoyable to work with.

This all took place either on tour, since I became a fixture on pre-season tours for the next few years, or back in the Carrington gym. It's a cliché which has been trotted out before, but the gaffer was always the first person in the building at Carrington. That meant that I would need to be in at the same time as him because he always had so much going on. He became very interested in staying in shape, but while he'd come in the gym relatively regularly, other times he'd arrange to come in but he'd end up being too busy.

* * *

The gaffer's role at United changed enormously over time. When he first arrived at the club in 1986, he had a very small number of staff and actually had to massage some of the players himself because they needed the treatment and the masseur couldn't do everybody at once. Over time, things began to grow and develop and he had to become a master delegator.

Through it all, his genius lay in one thing he couldn't delegate to anybody else: observing.

He was first in at Carrington because he would study people

as they arrived on the premises. From his office, he could read people's body language as they were coming into the building. He'd see who was coming in early or late, who had a spring in their step and who had the weight of the world on their shoulders. This applied to staff as well as players. With the players, he'd make his observations and then factor them into his thinking when training started. He'd go out and watch the session but seldom get too involved. He had coaches for that. His job had been done in the recruitment of the best coaches. His presence at training was simply to read the individuals and the collective.

He would observe his players and see who was at it in that moment; who was really on song and who wasn't. A game would come along and quite often some people would be up in arms about his team selection, trying to fathom what he was thinking because Player A should have been in ahead of Player B, but what they didn't know is that Player A had been having trouble at home and was out of sorts, whereas Player B had been flying in training for weeks. Player B tended to go on and prove to be an inspired selection.

The gaffer was constantly watching everybody and it wasn't just how they were playing, it was how they were acting. It was their energy levels and the vibes they were giving off. He was the best I've ever seen at reading people's behaviour and body language. He hardly ever stopped, either. People in football forever talk amongst themselves, and I've heard of several managers who loved having days off and would only turn up to the training ground two or three days a week. Sir Alex Ferguson was there virtually all the time, and the energy levels you need to do that are very, very high. He was always taking on new fuel all the time to do that. It didn't just dissipate. It's like a fire. Some fires don't go out, they find new fuel to burn and that's what he was like, in my eyes. He's not an ordinary man.

As well as a supreme motivator and leader, he's also a strategist. I know he used to read books on tactics from Roman battles, and he'd listen to audiobooks about the American Civil War, among other things. Conflicts and how to triumph within conflicts absolutely fascinated him.

Again, football people are always talking and you can never place total faith in what you've heard, but one rumour I heard about his brilliance – among the many – was that he had four TV sets in his front room so that he could watch four different games at the same time. I've never been to his house so I can't verify this, but it wouldn't surprise me at all if it were true. To do that, to watch individual players that he's interested in signing, or teams that he's about to face, simultaneously, would be multi-tasking on an unbelievably multifaceted scale.

The guy is so complex, with a brain functioning on a different level, but that kind of approach requires an awful lot of energy all the time, so it can take a toll.

That was well illustrated in early 2004. By this point I'd been training him for a little while, so I'd learnt to tune into him. One particular morning when we were training, I noticed something was off about him, and I asked him if he was ok.

"Yeah, but I feel as if something's not right," he said, so I had him sit on an exercise bike and put his hands on the heart monitors. I noticed the heart rate was shooting right up, then suddenly back down. Right up, then back down. I also got the impression he was going very red and then very white.

I said: "Looking at these heart rate monitors and looking

at you as you are, I don't think you're at your best, so we're going to have to be careful with your training."

I kept an eye on him and, over the course of days and weeks, just felt that something was still amiss, so I went to Mike Stone, the club doctor at the time, and the physio team, and I explained that something wasn't right with the gaffer. They weren't sure of the validity of the readings from the bike, so they suggested hooking him up to a proper heart monitor, which we did. The same thing happened with the readings going up and down, so again they weren't sure, but rather than blame the monitors I was quite clear to them: "I don't go off those readings, I go off what I'm seeing. Something's not right and I think he should be looked at."

Nothing was ever said to me, but he had a pacemaker fitted soon afterwards.

Once the heart condition had been recognised, I was on at him even more to look after himself. Because he didn't directly recruit me – Rob Swire did – I think I always felt a step removed from the backroom staff he'd built. That was good in the sense that it allowed me to be neutral in a lot of situations. Most people had an office; I had a desk in the gym. That's where anybody – staff or players – could come and talk to me, and I'd listen and give the advice I thought was right. I think I was very unusual around the place from that point of view. It also meant I could probably speak to Sir Alex in a different way to most of the others.

I'd bully him in a playful way. In the canteen I'd say: "Are you watching what you eat?" I would sometimes go up to him and if I could see he was hyper, I'd just grab his shoulders and give him a quick massage. He should have gone for more regular massages but he didn't like going to physios or doctors for help, so he had to make do with a couple of minutes from me every now and then. As I did it, you could feel the tension that his lifestyle was creating and you could hear him letting off steam as he exhaled. Probably because I was closer to him in age than most of his staff, I felt comfortable telling him off for his own good.

I was always moaning at him, especially after having the pacemaker fitted, so he lovingly began to call me by a new nickname.

Hitler.

He'd literally introduce me to his family and friends that way if he brought anybody into Carrington.

"This is Hitler. He runs the gym here."

"Gaffer, that's not really very nice," I'd protest. "Hitler was responsible for killing millions of people. I'm a nasty little bastard, but I'm not quite on those levels."

"Ah, but you would be if you'd had the chance. If they hadn't found that body in the bunker in Germany, I'd swear to you that this guy was Hitler."

That's how our relationship was. Because I was a little bit of an outsider, I couldn't say that I had a massively close relationship with him, but I felt he respected what I did and I most definitely respected what he did. We were able to function and do a good job together for a long, long time, and when I go back over the great privileges that my career has given me, there really aren't many better than getting to work with one of sport's greatest minds.

CHAPTER 16

Fabien
and Linda

*"I agreed and thought nothing more of it until,
after Barthez had left the room, someone else asked
me, 'You do know who his girlfriend is, right?'"*

Working for United would quite often put me in unusual situations.

Fabien Barthez, as most people will know, was barmy. All goalkeepers are perceived to be slightly odd in one way or another, but Fabien was a level above the rest. He was a nightmare for Tony Coton, our goalkeeping coach. Tony was there to improve Fabien as a goalkeeper, but there was one big problem: Fabien wanted to play outfield.

On the rare occasions I'd go out onto the training pitch during his time at the club, I'd usually see him playing outfield with the rest of the lads. He just didn't want to go in goal. At the end of the session, Tony was trying to get him to do some goalkeeping training. And Fabien would come up with excuses. Quite often, he'd say he needed to go to the gym. Before I saw him, he'd sneak off to see the staff in the laundry, have a coffee and come to see me smelling of smoke.

I got on very well with Fabien. He wasn't averse to doing work in the gym and he was in there quite a bit. One day he said to me: "Cleggy, my girlfriend bought a running machine and it's not working. Could you go and sort it out for her?"

I agreed and thought nothing more of it until, after Fabien had left the room, someone else asked me: "You do know who his girlfriend is, right?"

"Nope. Should I?"

"It's Linda Evangelista."

I didn't exactly have my finger on the pulse of pop culture, so I still had to Google her.

Wow. I was going to meet a supermodel.

A few days later, I went along to their place – a city centre apartment, just off Deansgate. I knocked on the door. Nothing happened. I knocked again.

The door opened and there stood an ordinary lady. No makeup, baggy clothes, very quiet. I'd been expecting the door to reveal this vision of beauty, but there were no white lights, no harps playing.

Ok, Linda must be inside, I thought.

The girl invited me in and started explaining the issues with the treadmill. She'd had it for a couple of years, it had been sent over from America, but it just hadn't worked since it arrived in Manchester.

Having been an electrician – among other things – in my younger years, I ventured that it was probably something to do with the plugs, going from 210V in America to 220-240V over here.

I got to work. While I was fixing it, I asked her: "So, you train here with Linda then?

"No, I am Linda."

Oh, for fuck's sake.

I attempted to play it down at first but then just came clean and said: "Sorry, this is me: I always put my foot in it."

Thankfully, she was absolutely fine with my mistake. Maybe it even broke the ice, because within long we got to chatting. I found Linda to be a really nice lady, very pleasant, very normal. I'd gone with these expectations of otherworldly experience, but in fact I had this completely different exchange. I did not see Linda Evangelista on that day as people see her on film or in magazines; I saw this other person. Scruffy clothes, mascara goop in her eyes, messy hair, but absolutely lovely to talk to. There are beautiful people who are ugly inside, but this wasn't the case with Linda. On that day it was the other way around.

It was a real eye-opener for me. I suppose I really should have learnt from my experiences with footballers that the person you see on screen or read about isn't always the real person. So we had a great chat, I managed to fix the treadmill and, before I left, she asked me if I would train her. As you can imagine, I left the place absolutely bemused by my first ever meeting with a supermodel.

A few days later, I was doing some one-on-one work with Giggsy in the gym and Fabien came in. He was bored, possibly frustrated because he hadn't played outfield in training that day, and he said to us: "I have a trick to show you."

I said: "Yeah, I've seen your trick: what Linda looks like behind closed doors, and what she looks like for the cameras!"

He laughed, then said: "No, watch this."

Outside the gym, Carrington had a big sports hall which had various uses. It was a huge space and I'd been in the middle of working with Ryan on his crossing. The coaches would play badminton in there, there was a table tennis table and there were also basketball nets which could be retracted. In this instance, they were folded up perpendicular to the roof, so the hoop was dangling down and facing us. Fabien looked at one of the nets, probably 60 feet away and at least 20 feet in the air. He turned to us.

"I'm going to put this ball through that hoop."

Giggsy and I just stood there laughing at him.

"You can't possibly do that."

This is the thing. What people say they're going to do and what they can actually do, they don't always correlate. This is the kind of situation where people show you what they're made of.

Nowadays, you can look around online and see people doing the most incredible things, but you're just seeing one successful instance of what they're trying to do. What you don't see is the hundreds of outtakes where they failed. They'll be filming all day, eventually what they're trying to do comes off once and they stick that on YouTube, TikTok or wherever.

Not Fabien.

Fabien walks into the sports hall, says: "I'm going to put this ball through that hoop."

He picks the ball up with one hand, hurls it towards the hoop, and through it goes. All net.

He didn't even stop to watch it go through. Didn't make sure it had gone in. Didn't gloat about it to us. He just started walking and never looked back. Just walked away.

Giggsy and I just laughed. It was seriously one of the most impressive things I've ever seen in my entire career.

* * *

When you actually sat down and studied Fabien's game, a big part of it was the ability to get the ball and quickly throw it accurately over long distances. Fabien would be watching everything that was going on, and people wouldn't always understand what he was doing with these theatrical dummies and feints that he was so fond of, but it's all about mathematics. He was weighing up the perfect player in the perfect position, then working angles and distances for throws or kicks to whichever team-mate was best placed. He was really, really accurate with his distribution.

Fabien would also get bored with just keeping goal. He played outfield in a pre-season friendly in Singapore once and he really fancied himself as a footballer. That was on show with the way he played – he would make a lot of work for himself around the 18-yard box, I reckon just to amuse himself a lot of the time.

He was a nightmare for Tony to coach because he would only give him 30 to 40 minutes a day on actual goalkeeping training. He'd come from Monaco, where training was done a lot differently to how things were at United at that time. There were problems trying to get what was required into Fabien because of a lack of understanding of what preparation was required. I think the ultimate end of Fabien came midway through his first full season at the club when we played West Ham in the FA Cup.

Paolo Di Canio went clean through and Fabien stood still

with his arm raised, trying to trick Di Canio into thinking that offside had been given. It didn't work, Di Canio scored and we went out of the FA Cup, and the manner of it really pissed the gaffer off. There were other instances which raised question marks, a couple of unfortunate mistakes in his second season, and I think they all combined to convince the gaffer to look elsewhere.

Replacing Peter Schmeichel, who left the club in 1999, had given United real issues. He was arguably the greatest goalkeeper in United's history, one of the best to play the game, so it was never going to be straightforward to follow him. When I arrived at the club, Mark Bosnich was no.1, but it didn't work out for him at all. The thing with Mark was that he had a personal trainer so he could do extra work on top of his day-to-day work with United, which was a great gesture and really showed that he had the determination to be as good as he could be, but the type of training he was doing was, in my opinion, detrimental to what he wanted to achieve.

He did a lot of heavy strength training, a lot of heavy squats and deadlifts. As a whole, the physio staff said they were quite dubious about what Mark was doing. It was too much about making muscle, about being strong and powerful rather than being fast and agile. I got on with Mark and I thought he was a very good goalkeeper too, but Tony Coton's coaching was all about movement, speed and agility, which was the case for my work as well. It was football-specific, whereas the strength-oriented work he was doing didn't suit his job. That's where your conditioning work can really work against you.

Mark came in as Schmeichel's replacement, but ended up sharing the job with Raimond van der Gouw, who was an absolutely brilliant trainer. He had an unbelievable physique; so lean, strong, powerful, quick. He trained very, very hard, always tried different things in the gym, always challenged us as coaches and questioned everything we did. He was another who loved the boxing; he was brilliant on the focus mitts. Unfortunately, he couldn't pin down the no.1 slot either, so the gaffer brought in Fabien. A year on, in came Roy Carroll to provide further competition but he never managed to fully convince the manager that he should start every game.

Even though we were still winning Premier League titles – 2000/01 and 2002/03, having finished third in 2001/02 – the gaffer still saw goalkeeper as a problem position, so he brought in young USA international Tim Howard, who was an unknown quantity in England, in the summer of 2003. This was ahead of the pre-season tour of the States, and while I was over there I got chatting with Bob Bradley, who was manager of New York MetroStars, Tim's former club. He asked me to go back over and do some work with them, so I returned for a couple of weeks later that year.

During that time, I met Mark Williams, who was Tim's strength and conditioning coach at the Metros. He shared tips and insights from his time working with Tim, who had adapted brilliantly to life in Manchester, both on the pitch and in the gym. He would really put the time in with his gym work. He was a really powerful guy, another keen boxer too, so his training was ferocious and tremendously enjoyable, especially with Mark's pointers.

Nevertheless, despite all his best efforts and that strong start, Tim ended up losing his place and sharing duties with Roy Carroll. With this uncertainty in goal and the loss of Rio Ferdinand to long-term suspension after missing a drugs test, we ended up finishing third again, 15 points off top spot. Though that was tempered slightly by winning the FA Cup, the manager had long since recognised that his squad was a work in progress whose best times lay ahead. Following David Beckham's departure to Real Madrid, Tim had joined alongside four other young newcomers in the summer of 2003: Kleberson, Eric Djemba-Djemba and David Bellion.

There was a young Portuguese lad, too...

CHAPTER 17

That Boy Ronaldo

"Ronaldo explained he had been sat in a hotel bar after the PFA awards and had been approached by an extremely attractive woman. They began talking and she complimented his body. At which point, Cristiano told me, he stood proud, struck a double bicep flex and simply said, 'Built by Cleggy.'"

One weekday morning in April 2007, I was milling about the gym at Carrington. I'd been there since 7.30am, as usual, and could always count on seeing certain players not long after that time each day. The correlation was usually quite simple: the better the player, the more time they spent doing extra work at the training ground, so they would arrive earlier and leave later than the majority of the squad.

Cristiano Ronaldo was always among the earliest to arrive, and on this particular morning he purposely caught my attention. With a smile on his face, he beckoned me to come and jog on the treadmill next to his.

Two nights previously, Cristiano had been in London to pick up one of his plentiful awards from the Professional

Footballers' Association. United were on the brink of winning the 2006/07 Premier League title and Ronaldo had been the star of the show all season long. Accordingly, he was named both senior and young player of the year, later going on to win awards from division sponsors Barclays and the Football Writers' Association to complete a clean sweep of the major individual honours on offer.

So awards dinners were nothing new to him. Neither were women. A handsome, athletic specimen permanently in the public eye – and a terrifically nice guy to boot – he lived his life under the constant glare of female attention. And so he had plenty of stories about women. On this particular day, for the first and only time, one of them also involved me.

As I began jogging next to him, he explained how he had been sat in a hotel bar after the PFA awards and had been approached by an extremely attractive woman. They began talking and, after a while, she started to compliment his body. At which point, Cristiano told me, he stood proud, struck a double bicep flex and simply said: "Built by Cleggy."

I was never quite sure what to make of the fact that he thought of me in that situation, and I had to wonder what his statement even meant to the woman in question, but on a purely professional level it was a pretty substantial compliment. It was untrue, of course: only one man built Cristiano Ronaldo and that is the man himself. Never before or since have I come across an athlete with such dedication and unyielding focus on wringing every last drop of potential from himself.

Some players, like Roy Keane, I remember the very first time I spoke to them in detail. That isn't the case with Cristiano. When he first joined the club back in 2003, he hung around the outskirts of the group, like most newcomers would. He was friends with another new signing, Kleberson, and Ricardo Lopez, a Spanish back-up goalkeeper who had been at the club for a year or so. In his first couple of sessions in the gym, Ronaldo was just quietly sussing things out and seeing what everybody did. Then, within his first week, we began to talk and we chatted about what he wanted to achieve. I asked him, in my usual abrupt fashion, why he was in the gym.

"I want to be the best. You will help me."

Now that, I liked.

* * *

There's a misconception that Cristiano arrived as a little skinny kid. He had a good physique when he started. He was only 18 and slim, but what he did well was take things steady; he didn't try to change things there and then. This is a big part of Ronaldo's success: he was patient. He knew where he was going and that it would take him time to get there. He didn't make any secret of the fact that he wanted to be the best player in the world; he would proclaim long and loud, with complete confidence, that he was going to do so, even within a few months of joining United.

He was a very, very strong character. Strong in the fact that he felt he was doing everything right. He had plenty of coaches to tell him what he needed to do, and I never really made it my business to talk about football with the players, but one thing I did say to him during the course of our friendship was an overview of the situation he had arrived in. His early form was good, but inconsistent, and I felt he needed to hear context so that he could understand his situation within the collective. After we had bonded and could chat regularly, he came and sat on my desk in the gym one day, having had fairly regular criticism from both inside and outside the club for his perceived showboating and his work as an individual, rather than a team player. The point I made to him was that he had to remember who he had taken over from. David Beckham looked after Gary Neville for years and he was a workaholic up and down that right flank; he defended as much as he attacked, and I explained that to Cristiano. I told him that yes, he had to score goals, make chances for others and all the rest of it, but he had to defend as well, and he didn't know that side of the game; he didn't think that was what he had to do. That's a real thing that he had to learn, but he only took a small part of it on.

Then, because he wasn't prepared to do all that, he had to make himself even better than he was, and that was the thing. He realised: *I can't do what David Beckham did. I'm not David Beckham. I've got to go my way and do it my way without the support of a lot of people.* In training, some of his team-mates were shouting: "You're not getting the ball in the fucking box. That's your job, not trying to fucking score all the time or show off your fucking fancy tricks. Get the ball, see me and get it to me." The fact is, Cristiano initially struggled with that side of the game, with actually understanding how it would be seen from another point of view.

Ronaldo was very focused, and focus can give you tunnel-vision. But it didn't need to. Being focused on something doesn't mean you have to lose your overall sight. I think in some ways he had to say to himself: *I've got to do it differently to how others are doing it. That is not my way. I've got to make myself even better than I should be because I'm not prepared to comply*. And that's how he struggled with all sorts of different people telling him to do this and do that. He didn't always get picked in his first few years at the club and he lost form, but what did he do?

He didn't worry about it or get scared about it; he knew his own potential. If you go into games in the Premier League or Champions League, you're constantly testing yourself, and he had the brains and the balls to think: It's not quite going right here so I've got to do *this* instead, and that's why every day he would devote his time at the training ground to improving himself.

The very best players do extra work to improve themselves; that's a simple fact. Nobody is a better example of the rewards of labour than Ronaldo. I would regularly say that, and it got me into trouble with a few of the players because I was so public in my praise of him. They saw in an interview I did with United's monthly magazine that I had labelled Cristiano the most intelligent player at the club because he wanted it more than anyone else. That didn't go down well with everybody. But whether they liked it or not, it was a fact. When it came to wanting to work, he was the most insistent player I've ever worked with. His overall attitude was 'I need, I want' and he was prepared to listen that little bit more than the other players.

Only small amounts, but that's what made him the best: he did the most. Some players arguably had as much natural talent – perhaps even more – but didn't match Cristiano's dedication to self-improvement, so they plateaued while he continued a steady ascent.

It wasn't rocket science. It was very formulaic. He went on to become this frightening football beast at Real Madrid, and an incredible physical specimen, and people would often ask me about him and say to me that I helped change him from a skinny little wimp into a massive powerful guy, but that was never the case. If you look back at pictures of him over the years, you see that development. It's purely through him insisting on getting the right stuff at the right time and building over a period of time.

We worked on loads of different things. Obviously there were some basics. He liked his body and he liked to have a highly defined mid-section, so he worked hard at it. I would work out with all the players when I did one-on-one sessions with them, so I used to have a bloody good body, just from training with him every day. I was in my mid-40s, but because of him I was in terrific shape!

One day he'd do his upper body, one day he'd do mid-section, another day he'd do legwork, another day he'd do fast feet work, other days it'd be sprints and power jumps, so his week would be absolutely full. The players could be playing Tuesday-Saturday-Wednesday-Saturday, so these sessions were always slotted into the schedule only where they were possible. He was so insistent that he wanted absolute conditioning that I used to be very careful with what he did.

United had been so successful for all those years, even though the club's approach to rest was fairly old school. Sir Alex Ferguson liked to have the day after a game off, so that's the way it had always been. Ronaldo was one of those who would always be in and we'd have set patterns of training to go with his football, but we had a level of trust whereby either of us could insist on something to the other. Sometimes when he walked through the gym door, I'd look at him and say: "Cristiano, fuck off." I looked into his eyes, looked at his body, realised what he was doing training-wise and in games and was able to say: "I don't think you should train." Or, I'd say: "You lazy bastard, get in that fucking gym." He would accept either. If I told him to leave, he'd just go away, no problem. What was the point in me being there as an advisor or a coach if they weren't listening? I trusted him to do the right thing for himself and he trusted me to do the right thing for him.

Cristiano's training was all football specific – plus a little extra mid-section work because he wanted it – so he micro-managed his physique, but also his performance, which was massively important to his development. Outside the canteen window at Carrington, there are a series of small hills which shield a flat area of grass so nobody can see it. And he would go off to that area and practise on his own.

He didn't want anybody there, didn't want a coach or the manager there. He didn't want any feedback from anybody else because he knew what he was doing and he knew whether he was doing it right or wrong. The manager didn't even know he was doing it – and I found this out because one day the gaffer came to me in the gym with a bone to pick.

"Ronaldo's injured and he's been injured in the gym," he said, matter-of-factly. "He hasn't been injured out there during training; I watched him, so he's done it in the gym."

I said: "It's interesting, that, because he's not done anything in here that I think could have given him an injury, just like you haven't seen him do anything out on the training pitch. But what about the other place he goes?"

"What do you mean?"

"Where he does a lot of his work."

"What are you talking about?"

Where my coaching journey began. Outside Ashton Old Baths, where I first entered the taekwondo gym all those years ago

t was a journey that saw me build professional relationships with the biggest talents in the game – Cristiano Ronaldo was the heart and soul of he gym for years. Quite simply, he wanted it more than anyone else

I soon realised that boxing was an excellent way to connect with the United players. Scholesy wasn't the most powerful, but he was gifted in other ways

John O'Shea, Giggsy, Wes Brown, Edwin van der Sar and Wayne Rooney were all great to work with as individuals – here I am leading them on a warm-up during a pre-season trip to Japan in 2007

Gary Neville enjoyed a stint on the pads – he also enlisted me to help with his guitar-playing at one point...

I almost got off on the wrong foot with Rio Ferdinand, but we ended up having a fantastic relationship after a rocky start

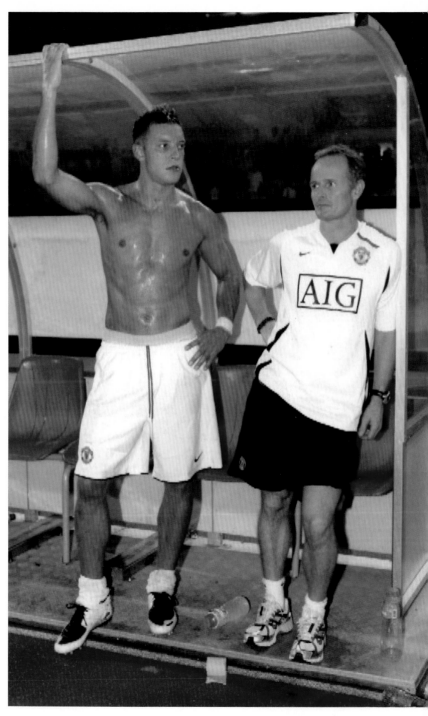

I got on brilliantly with Alan Smith – but he suffered a horrible injury at Anfield and he was never the same player again physically

HALLO KLEINE MIK
BEDANKT VOOR
AL JE TIJD EN INZET

E VD SAR.

United winning the Champions League in 2008 was a true milestone. At the after-party, Edwin van der Sar thanked me for all my hard work by picking me up and trying to fit me inside the European Cup

After I left United, Darren Fletcher sought me out for help during his battle with ulcerative colitis. I was so proud when he returned to the United first team after a long absence

Ryan Giggs was the benchmark in the United squad – and he was always open to new ideas which could help him prolong his career

I put the squad through their paces at Nike HQ in Portland, Oregon, on United's pre-season tour of 2003

Working with taekwondo star Aaron Cook. We managed to add a touch of aggression to his performances, helping him to win medals on the international stage

Getting on the pads with Tameside kickboxer Mike Eade

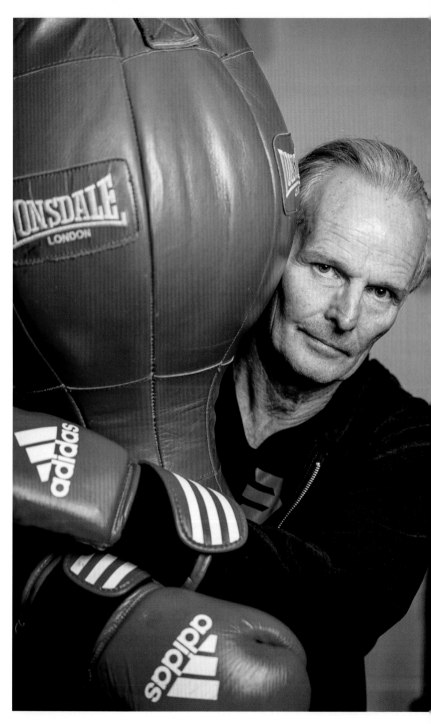

What a journey it's been – and I've still got plenty left in the tank for some sparring!

"Come on, boss. You know Ronaldo always goes and does his own training over the other side of that hill. He practises running with the ball and doing skills with the ball and crossing the ball, all on his own. He tries things, tries to perfect what he does. There's a good chance he could have hurt himself out there while he was trying something."

"Ah, ok."

And he just walked out. The manager would look out onto the training pitch and watch everything that was going on, both during the session and as the players were coming back in. There were lots of players milling around, and Ronaldo was able to disappear in the crowd, then go and do his own work behind the hills. A lot of the other players and staff didn't see him. I knew, because I knew that he would come into the gym about 25 minutes after everybody else.

He wasn't the first player to disappear in that gap between training and the gym – Fabien Barthez used to nip for a fag in the laundry room before his gym training – but Cristiano would work on his own, then come straight in the gym and do his routine with me.

Those sessions spent alone were absolutely key to what he did. He would work on something by himself – a new trick, for instance – without any pressure, then slip it into training to put it to the test against his team-mates, then work it into small games, then into big games. You're building and learning and it all fits together in the end. That was part of a decision he arrived at when he concluded: *I'm not going to be David Beckham and work my arse off for Gary Neville. I'm Ronaldo, I'm special. I'm going to prove I'm special.* He knew he had to work so much harder to prove that he was special, so there was no use in him just saying it and thinking it; he had to prove it by doing it and then implementing it in his game because that's where it counted.

It took time, of course. As crazy as it sounds with hindsight, we didn't always think he was going to make it at United. I spent a lot of time talking about it with Jim Ryan, another member of the coaching staff. Ronaldo was paid a lot of money, came for a big fee and in the eyes of many he should have been the real deal straight away, but it took time. He had problems with being kicked by opponents, he didn't fully win over all his new team-mates and it did take time for all his practice to come together into a tangible end product.

But while Cristiano's assimilation took a little time on the field, it was a different story off it. He was both very confident and very intelligent, and he was also perhaps helped by the changing make-up of the United squad at the time. He was sharp, witty and very, very clever. He was multilingual.

I remember being in a lift with him and a variety of players during one of the club's pre-season tours of Asia. Cristiano was speaking to Nani in Portuguese, then to another player in another language and one of the English lads piped up and jokingly told him to speak English. Ronaldo made the point that he could speak four languages, and the English's problem was that, as a nation, they only speak the one.

It was key that Ronaldo could communicate with players from different backgrounds in an increasingly cosmopolitan squad. In the year or two prior to his arrival, the English-speaking core at United had lost a few characters – Beckham, of course, plus Dwight Yorke, Andy Cole, David May, Denis Irwin and Jaap Stam – and Cristiano's ability to converse with lots of players allowed him to quickly grow into a big personality in the evolving dressing room.

Personally, I thrived on the professional challenge of working with Cristiano. He was a terrific lad and always good company, but he constantly pushed boundaries and challenged me as a coach. In terms of all the athletes I've worked with, he's probably been the most important in my career. His development as a player converged with my development as a coach. You never stop learning, and I learnt so much from working with somebody imbued with such drive and single-mindedness in the pursuit of some exceptionally ambitious goals.

It all came together for him, of course. Ronaldo achieved his aim of becoming the world's best player and won his first Ballon d'Or at United, and then went on to reach stupendous heights at Real Madrid. His time with us was vital in his development because he'd really gone as far as he could with United. While he perfected everything in the lower games, he didn't produce the goods consistently in the big games until the very end of his time at Old Trafford because he wasn't quite ready. It wasn't all solidified in that brain of his. He was ready for the next step and once he got to Real Madrid he showed the football world just what he could do.

Him being him, he was never satisfied and he continued to improve out in Spain. He went on to win a spate of Ballon d'Ors and European honours, and he remained insatiable in his pursuit of more glory. That's what he's good at: fine tuning and adjustments to make himself special and keep getting even better. I've not come across anybody like him and to this day I still get asked about working with him more than any other player. I imagine I will always regard it as the greatest privilege of my career to have worked with such a player, such a man, at such an important stage in his development.

CHAPTER 18

The Benchmark

"Giggy excelled with 'the whacker'... The concept was as cutting-edge as it sounds: you use the whacker to whack people in the stomach, and they absorb the blows. Of course, you don't just sashay into Carrington, beckon Roy Keane or Paul Scholes over and start smacking them in the gut..."

When Cristiano Ronaldo came to United, it was obvious that he was a man on a mission: becoming the best player in the world. It didn't take him long to figure out the first step towards achieving that at United: becoming better than Ryan Giggs.

Cristiano spent time studying how all the other players in the squad approached their preparation, and it only took him a couple of weeks to realise that Giggsy was the benchmark on that score. Ryan's dedication at that time was second to none.

I spent over a decade working at United, but Ryan was in the first team for a decade before I arrived and he remained one of the best players in the team until he retired three years after I'd gone. That kind of longevity is absolutely freakish, and it's a huge part of the reason he was able to amass more honours in his career than most clubs have picked up in their entire history.

In terms of my own interactions with him, Ryan stands out as the most trainable player I ever worked with. He was absolutely open-minded when it came to anything at all which could help him keep improving as a footballer, and he would trust the experts around him who he felt could facilitate that. He worked wonders for my career.

Bear in mind that when he started, it was even before the Premier League was formed, before football became a really big business full of off-field investment. Preparation then wasn't anything like what it is now, so Ryan had no model to work from. He became the model. He set the standards from the first day that I walked into that gym. He was absolutely perfect to work with.

He would try virtually anything. He would look at it, talk to people about it and then try it. It's almost like going through different doors with him. There's an idea; let's open the door. Now let's talk to the person on the other side of the door. If they're talking sense then we'll go through the next door, where we actually try it out.

For me, that was absolutely ideal. I maintain to this day that creativity is one of the most important aspects of coaching, and I was constantly looking for new ideas or new angles on old ideas. Working with players like Giggsy, Roy and the others meant that I was challenged every single day. Once you win over a player of that calibre and standing, you don't just stand still and keep doing the same thing. You need to be constantly evolving and striving, as they were, or they would quickly discover that you weren't up to the job at hand. It takes a lot of time and effort to win the trust of top-level athletes, but it's a far quicker process to lose that trust. Being creative is crucial. If you just do the same as everyone else then you can only hope to be in the top bracket. If you do something completely different, however, you're going to be a different player. Ryan was one of those who was always pushing for new and different approaches. He came up to me in the gym, around the start of the 2002/03 season, and just asked: "Right, what have you got for me?"

As ever, consultation was key, so I asked him what one aspect of his game he really wanted to improve, more than any other. Quick as a flash, he had his answer.

"Crossing. I would *love* my crossing to be better."

He carried on and explained that he wanted to be able to get his left foot in exactly the right place as he crossed, having gotten to the byline. Having seen a lot of him in action already by that stage, I tended to agree. He could beat opponents for pace or dribble by them for fun, but the consistency of his crossing didn't match up to the stellar work that would get him into position to cross. Looking back, he was getting plenty of assists, but very, very few of them came from crosses which, for a winger, wasn't ideal.

So I looked at him and I don't know how it came to me, but I just said: "Right Ryan, go over there to my desk and write your autograph on a piece of paper." He laughed at me. Again, I said: "Go on, just go over there and write something." So he walked over and started writing with his right hand.

In general, left-footed people are left-handed and right-footed people are right-handed. I looked at him writing with his right hand and it just didn't seem right, so I said: "Right, now write with your left hand," and I honestly believe, purely in my personal opinion, that it looked more natural to him when he was writing with his left hand, even though he'd never done it.

By that stage, I was studying a lot about the machinations of the brain and the way to achieve perfect balance. As he was right-handed he probably wasn't using his left arm as much as he should, and I theorised that if he started using it more then he'd probably find that it would be able to give him more power to drive, to get more from his body and to get the ball over better.

So I told him: "The way I see it is, you're a left-sided person who's writing and doing lots of other things with your right hand. That approach has been in place from your youth. I reckon that if we worked on your left-hand side, it'll give you better balance in your brain and body and you'll become better at crossing a ball."

Not every player would have gone for that, let me tell you, but Ryan actually took me up on it. Since I was still in my relatively early days of coaching at United, it was fantastic to get a guy like that, who'd won everything, taking me up on what sounded like a theoretical punt.

So, in order to get both sides of his body working on a more even keel, we had to get him using his left hand more often. As ever, it helped to make it sports-relevant, so that his hand-eye coordination developed quickly, and competitive, so that it would appeal to the winner in him. That meant that for a period of a few weeks, every time Ryan came into the gym, he'd do his usual workout and then tag on an extra session aimed at restoring his balance.

As bizarre as it sounds, that would involve the pair of us playing darts or table tennis in the Carrington gym. I could play as I normally would, but Giggsy had to use his left hand.

Naturally, it took him a little bit of getting used to, as his brain opened up the required neural pathways, but within a couple of sessions he was absolutely hammering me at whatever we played.

The approach was clearly working in the arena of those sports, but Ryan wasn't a left-handed professional playing darts or table tennis. He was a left-footed footballer, so we needed to see what – if any – changes were taking place with his crossing. I supplemented the regime with a routine which wasn't especially popular with any of the other staff at the training ground, because it involved that weird little fella from the gym taking over the entire sports hall.

I'd grab a fit ball – the large inflatable balls that are used for yoga, stability exercises, abs work and so on, maybe three times as a big as a football – and stand in the middle of the sports hall. I had Ryan run with a football at his feet, until he was maybe 15 or 20 yards away, stood parallel to me, at which point I'd throw the fit ball up in the air to provide him a target, which he then had to hit by crossing the football.

That probably sounds simple, but it's very difficult to do and when we first started, Giggsy struggled to hit the fit ball very often, maybe three or four times out of 10. As the weeks progressed, however, with more practice, with more left-handed sports, his numbers shot up and he reached the point where he was hitting the ball literally nine times out of 10. Other players, of course, spotted what he was doing and started joining in to see how they got on in comparison, but nobody ever came close to Ryan's nine out of 10. I'm not sure anybody else ever topped five.

As fun and interesting as all of this was, it would have been completely pointless if it hadn't translated into results on the pitch. Thankfully, within six to seven weeks of starting the regime, Ryan's crossing had become deadly during games. Between my arrival in 2000 and the summer of 2002, he'd assisted four goals with what would be regarded as orthodox crosses.

After we started specifically working on that area of his game, he got seven assists with crosses during the course of the 2002/03 season, including an absolutely exquisite one for a priceless goal by Scholesy at Tottenham which virtually won us the league. So, when everybody could see that our work was yielding almost twice the output in half the time, that vouched for the approach we'd taken. Amidst all of this, I had also suggested to Ryan that he should try yoga as he looked to get away from the injury issues which had affected his hamstrings in particular.

During my time trying meditation and hypnosis, long before coming to United, I'd done yoga myself. In its purest form, I didn't feel it was an especially good fit for footballers, so I put together my own kind of stretching which worked for the lads. Ryan felt he could go further and deeper into those stretches, so, after consulting with physio Neil Hough, I sourced a few yoga teachers and we got in someone called Louise McMullan. He worked with her brilliantly, then later her successor, Sarah Ramsden, and he went on to have a real affinity for yoga – to the point that he released a yoga DVD later in his career!

Nobody ever has a 100 percent success rate, however, so there were naturally things that I tried which Giggsy ultimately rejected. When he was in his mid-30s – either 34 or 35 – he used to get a lot of knee problems. I wanted him to be able to develop power but without pounding his knees, so trampolining seemed perfect. Sure enough, he was open to it. I did my research, located one of the best teachers in the area and took Ryan along to a gymnastics club in Salford. The guy made a mistake, however, by trying to show off how great trampolining was, so he had Giggsy hurtling 20 feet up in the air, rather than easing him in.

If you drop from that height and end up hurting yourself, especially in your mid-30s, it could be game over, and I could see Ryan thinking that he might injure himself, so trampolining never made its way into his routine.

* * *

There was a sweet spot in determining a training method's suitability, as far as Giggsy was concerned. He had the understanding and strength of character to decide that if something didn't challenge him mentally or physically then it was a waste of time, but it also had to be safe at all times. A big part of his longevity was his ability to manage his body and recognise what it needed at different times. He reached a point where he was putting some things into his routine and taking others out.

Over time he didn't do as much boxing or reaction work. He scaled back speed, reactions, twisting and turning. Sprinting and acceleration were providing him with pains after games, because of course there's a lot of pounding, and he didn't need to prove his speed to anyone. He'd shown his speed during games time and time again down the years, so there was no sense in making him sprint through test gates at Carrington. Throw a ball on a pitch when there was a goal to go for and then he was still unbelievably quick, but his training became more about being able to see things far better than others. As he started to move back into midfield, he reminded me of Rio with the way that he could just see what was happening long before others could. With that, his experience, his knowledge of the game and his physical mastery, he was able to flit between different positions even in his late 30s.

In terms of the secrets to Giggsy's football success and the role that gym work played in it, it's quite a boring answer: he was better than anybody at turning up on a regular basis and doing stuff in good, regimented segments. People come to the gym, then miss a few days, then a couple of weeks, but Giggsy was regimented. He wanted to get everything in place. He was the architect of his own body from the first day I started working with him until the last.

When you look at the reaction work we did, Scholesy was the best. Roy was the best at boxing. Rio had the strongest upper body. Ryan was doing all the same work as everyone else and he wasn't the best at one specific discipline, but he was among the best at everything, and if you reach that position then you can be the best overall.

Giggsy's body fat levels were incredible – around eight percent – and he loved mid-section work. He really liked having a good mid-section and had probably the best of the lot in my early years at the club. He excelled with 'the whacker', which was basically a big pad I used in boxing training at Olympic. The concept was as cutting-edge as it sounds: you use the whacker to whack people in the stomach, and they tense themselves and absorb the blows. Of course, you don't just sashay into Carrington, beckon Roy Keane or Paul Scholes over and start smacking them in the gut with this thing, so I had to introduce it gently.

That meant letting them use the whacker on me, so there was a queue of them taking turns smashing me in the stomach with it. As I was accustomed to the ways of the whacker after years of boxing training, I didn't move. When the roles reversed and I was able to introduce the whacker to the players, Giggsy was the one who was able to really tense his mid-section so it didn't hurt him.

With his dedication to regular training, his desire to be the best he could be and his ability to excel at virtually every discipline in the gym, Ryan was the benchmark for years. That's why, when Cristiano came, he looked at Ryan, turned to me and said: "I've got to be better than that."

Ryan was brilliant for my career, and I think he recognised that, however much I had helped him, he'd more than returned the favour by being open and receptive to my methods, which bought me credence with the other players and allowed me to cement myself in the backroom staff. So as I mentioned earlier, when Cristiano had been at the club for a couple of years, I was interviewed by United's club magazine and they asked which player was most dedicated to becoming the best professional footballer. I named Cristiano and that really pissed Ryan off at the time.

We had words about it. I regretted that because I genuinely appreciate Giggsy's role in my career, but I gave an honest answer based on what I saw: Ronaldo was in the gym the earliest and left the latest, and he always did extra work out of hours. Had I thought to expand my answer, I'd have explained that Ryan had been the benchmark for so long and had scaled back his work in order to fit in with his needs as an older player in the squad, whereas Cristiano was much younger and was making his way ferociously, relentlessly towards his aim of becoming the best player in the world. They were both doing what was right for them at their respective stages of their respective careers.

As I said earlier, when Ryan started out on his path in football, there was no example. By the time Cristiano began his own journey, he knew that all he had to do was follow Giggsy and he'd be on the right road.

CHAPTER 19

Total Footballer

"Wayne would say to me, 'Come on Cleggy, get the pads on,' and we'd do a boxing session in front of everybody... My word, he would throw some bloody punches in."

In 2013, I ended up on page three of *The Sun* because of Wayne Rooney. I could never have anticipated writing that sentence, nor could I have imagined it would be true, but it is completely accurate.

It followed my first (and last) interview with that newspaper, and I was double-crossed by underhanded reporting. I was asked to contribute to a general piece about pre-season training, which I did, answering questions about various topics which included Wayne Rooney and Cristiano Ronaldo. When I was asked to compare the training methods of the two, I gave them my opinion, which was that Rooney was lagging Ronaldo. I added that every player I had worked with fell into that category, such was Cristiano's supreme dedication, but I was still aware that the comments could be twisted, so I asked to see the finished piece before it went to print.

Later that day I was emailed the article, which was still a general look at pre-season training, but given that my quotes about Wayne were open to misinterpretation, I requested that they be removed. I didn't hear from the journalist again.

The next morning, I was quickly made aware that an entirely different article had made it into print; one which focused entirely on Wayne's fitness, linking my quotes to recent stories about his eating habits and generally framing him as lazy. It's safe to say that, since then, I've learnt my lesson about who I give interviews to and my insistence on copy approval.

With this episode in mind, I should tread very carefully and make my stance on Wayne very clear. He is one of the most naturally gifted footballers this country has produced. As far as I am aware, he preferred playing football on the training pitch to doing work in the Carrington gym. That's not unusual for a footballer – not many see the gym as a source of enjoyment.

With Wayne, he also had to consider the factor that his natural frame is very powerful and he had very legitimate concerns of bulking up too much if he spent too much time in the gym. That would have been detrimental to his performance on the pitch, which went against the point of our role on the fitness side of the club.

Wayne did apply himself to the gym, but just not as much as Ronaldo. But then, as I have already said, nobody did. Wayne is alongside Roy Keane, David Beckham, Ryan Giggs and whoever else you care to name because nobody is the equal of Ronaldo. There is no crime in putting in less gym time than Ronaldo because, from my experience, all other footballers fall into that category.

Rooney joined United a year after Cristiano, in the summer of 2004, and he was injured when he arrived, having broken a metatarsal bone in his right foot while playing for England at Euro 2004. He was desperate to get fit so he could make his debut, which he did in style by scoring a hat-trick against Fenerbahce, but it was always that kind of motivation which brought out the best in Wayne in the gym.

The thing about Rooney is that he's total-football. I always tried to give players opportunities to see me early doors after they'd joined the club. I'd always be at my desk in the gym anyway because you cannot build relationships with players when you're sat in an office. Wayne would come and wander around Carrington and just chat with the staff. He always went to the laundry ladies or he'd go and see our chef, Mike Donnelly, in the canteen because he needed to talk to normal folk. It's hard for those like Wayne who are in the public eye from such a young age, because they can't go out like ordinary people without being mithered for autographs or pictures.

So when he came to me and I asked him about his previous experience of gym training, the gist of his response was that he'd get ready, run round a bit and then play football, mainly five-a-side or six-a-side, then bugger off home afterwards. He said: "All I did was play football, because I'm a footballer." Thankfully, he also added: "I used to go with my brother to boxing, so I've done some boxing." From my point of view, I was now used to boxing with top-level footballers and that gave us an opportunity to build a relationship. Now, he never came in the gym a great deal, but when he did he wanted to do the boxing, that was the main thing. By God, was he powerful. So bloody powerful, he really was.

I found that to my cost on one occasion. Over time he developed a part of his routine which was slightly akin to Roy Keane, but manifested itself in a different manner. At

Carrington, the first port of call before group training was the sports hall, where 24 exercise bikes would be lined up for the squad to do their activation work before heading out onto the grass. The players would all sit there in the morning and pedal together in order to get their activation done as a group. Wayne would say to me: "Come on Cleggy, get the pads on," and we'd do a boxing session in front of everybody.

This started around late 2007. Roy had left the club in November 2005 and Wayne had been there for a few years by that point, and he was sending a very, very clear message to the rest of the players: *I'm the hard man here.* You've got Ronaldo sat at the back, alongside Nani and the rest, and Wayne would purposely do it in front of them, showing them what he was capable of. My word, he would throw some bloody punches in.

Whenever I do a boxing session with an athlete, I'm always telling them what to do, so I say 'jab', 'hook' and so on. Standard stuff. As the coach you've got to lead it, otherwise you can get severely hurt. On this particular day, Wayne and I were stood in front of everybody, he was obviously on a high because he swung a hook when I didn't ask for one. He hit me right across the jaw and cheekbone, and he really put everything into it. The whole lot of them just stopped pedalling as he hit me square across the face. I was amazed. I looked at him and thought: *I can't believe I'm still standing.*

I'd been totally unprepared for it and he'd put all his power into the hit. It all happened so quickly that I've no idea how he didn't just knock my head clean off. It was just a freak, a one-off event for me to still be standing after that. Obviously, he was surprised too, and for that moment nobody moved or spoke. After a second or two, I just leant over, put my hand on his shoulder and said: "Now you fucking behave yourself; just be careful what you're doing," I had a bit of nerve to say that, in retrospect, but then I owed him one – he had just punched me in the face!

* * *

Boxing and deadlines really brought out the best in Wayne. Just like his debut had come after a serious injury, he suffered another broken metatarsal at the end of the 2005/06 season which left his participation at the 2006 World Cup in doubt. At that time I was already working on the rehabilitation of Alan Smith, who had suffered an horrific broken leg and dislocated ankle a few weeks earlier, and Wayne put in an unbelievable amount of effort and time to join us and get fit for England. The motivation of making sure he didn't miss the World Cup changed Wayne's attitude to gym work because, in a short-term sense, it was do or die. In those circumstances, Wayne showed himself to be an amazing athlete. There is no question at all that he is an elite specimen.

Nevertheless, that was repeatedly questioned by the press. The English media has this obsession with Wayne because of his status as the country's leading light, so he has had to carry the can for a lot of the collective's continued failings. When he did make it to the 2006 World Cup, he infamously received a red card against Portugal for stamping on Ricardo Carvalho – though he maintained his innocence – and Cristiano got involved in apparently trying to get the referee to send Rooney off.

The media loved that. Not only did it give them a high-profile figure to bear the brunt of England's exit, but you had the two outstanding young players of Manchester United at loggerheads. It made for great reading, but certainly I can say that I never saw a single shred of evidence of a rivalry between them during their time together at Carrington. As is often the way, whether it was true or not, thereafter it became assumed knowledge that Cristiano and Wayne were rivals rather than team-mates, so any opportunity to compare the two was gleefully seized upon. I even tried it myself one day in the gym. Cristiano had just been named the world's number one player in *FourFourTwo* magazine's annual top 100 ranking. Wayne was some way down the list, around the mid-20s, I think. As usual at Carrington we had free copies of the magazine lying around reception, I grabbed one, spotted the ranking and showed it to Wayne. I asked him what he thought of it and he just shrugged and said he wasn't bothered by it.

"If you spent more time in the gym with me, put in extra time on the training field and matched Ronaldo's dedication, you could be in the top 10, top five, top three," I said. But he just said that it didn't matter, it was only a daft magazine poll and, at the end of the day, he was a footballer and all he wanted to do was play football.

I couldn't argue with his opinion; it reflects the way I have approached my own profession. People have tried to encourage me to do different things that they think might help me improve the way I work, but at the end of the day I'm just a coach. That's all I am and I stick to what I know.

I'll always wonder about that percent or two of extra work that Wayne might have put into his training, but the facts bear themselves out. He is an elite athlete, a stone-cold winner dripping in medals and he has the incredible honour of being the all-time leading goalscorer for England and Manchester

United. He is a diamond of a lad who has nothing to prove to anybody and I hope he eventually gets the recognition his career deserves.

CHAPTER 20

Hits And Misses

"Forlan was frightened to death. Imagine that: a United striker killing someone with a bow and arrow! Imagine the newspaper headlines. On the other side of the coin, there's somebody out there who may have spent years wondering who on earth would vandalise their brand-new BMW in 2003."

As a coach, you want to inspire your athletes. You want them to take on board what you're saying and act accordingly. That is, as long as it doesn't end up inspiring them to endanger human life.

I got on brilliantly well with Diego Forlan – as everyone did, to be fair, as he was such a great lad. One summer, I think it was 2003, everybody came back into Carrington for the start of pre-season training and, naturally, the chatter was around what everyone had done with their time off. There weren't any international tournaments, so everybody had been able to get in some proper rest.

Diego and I were discussing our respective breaks. He'd gone home to Uruguay, whereas the outstanding memory of my summer was taking our Shaun to an indoor shooting range. He liked rifles already but because he enjoyed himself so much, I ended up trying to develop things and bought him a bow and arrow set and a crossbow. It was only a small one, but it had proper arrows which could do some real damage if misused. There used to be a 60-metre run cordoned off on one side of Olympic where people could train for sprinting or hurdles, so I set up a target there after everyone had gone home and let Shaun try target practice. He was brilliant. He was only 11 or 12 but he could shoot very accurately.

Diego loved the notion of it – especially as a marksman by trade – so a few days later he came back into the gym and said: "Mick, I went shopping and got myself a bow, arrows and a target. When you told me about your son I had to go and buy some."

He had quite a nice long garden, so he planned to practise there. He was a total novice, though, so we had a long discussion about best practice: where and how he had to stand, what other factors he had to consider, and then off he went and I gave it no more thought.

A few days later, very early in the morning, I suddenly became aware of a very animated Diego knocking on the glass doors at the back of the gym.

"Let me in, let me in."

"What the hell's up with you?"

"I can't believe what's happened."

"What?"

"I've been getting really strong with the bow and arrow. Yesterday afternoon after training I got them out, set up the target, I was shooting and I let one go too far. It went way over the target, straight over the fence and into the fucking street."

Now, these arrows could maim you at short range if they hit

you in the wrong place. Fired powerfully from distance, they could easily kill you.

Diego had a half-smile on his face, but his eyes were wide with fear as he carried on recounting his story.

"I ran and jumped up onto the fence, I'm looking around and thinking: *I'm going to find somebody fucking dead here,* and I'm running around the street but I couldn't find it. There was nobody around but I knew I had to find it.

"I'm planning out where it could have gone, and as I'm walking back there was a brand-new BMW and the arrow had gone right through the headlamp, and all you could see was the feathers of the arrow. I'm looking around and I'm so happy that I haven't killed anybody, but there's a brand-new BMW with a fucking arrow through it. I'm trying to pull it out and a car comes around the corner, so I just ran, jumped over the fence, got the bow and the other arrows and put them in the garage. I'm never using them again!"

He was manic. We absolutely pissed ourselves about it but he was frightened to death, and I don't blame him. Imagine that: a United striker killing someone with a bow and arrow! Imagine the newspaper headlines if he hadn't been so lucky. On the other side of the coin, there's somebody out there who may have spent years wondering who on earth would vandalise their brand-new BMW in 2003. Now, the truth is out there.

Diego was at United for two-and-a-half seasons, having come in to provide more competition for Ruud and Ole. Coley had left and the writing was on the wall for Yorkie, so this relatively unheard-of youngster came in from Uruguay and was soon catching the eye in training. Diego was sharp, energetic and two-footed – a real handful for anybody he was up against. He was also beloved off the pitch. Everyone recognised that, as talented as he was, he was at United to graft, which was a sure-fire way to impress. He worked ever so hard at his English as well and that helped further with his integration.

The problem was that, as a striker, he was bought to score goals, but it took him 27 appearances to score for the first time. His rate picked up after that and he ended up basically averaging a goal every five games, but when he left in 2004 to join Villarreal, he set La Liga on fire. He was a sensation out there and went on to have a really good career.

He wasn't the first or the last who did well away from the pressure of being at United. A high number of players either joined from elsewhere or came up through the ranks in-house with huge potential but ended up failing to have the expected impact at first-team level. From my experience, I don't think it's pressure from the fans or the manager or their team-mates; it's all in their own mind. If a player came to Carrington and matched the effort levels around him, that was usually enough to appease the fundamental requirements of the squad and staff. Lazy sods needn't apply.

The majority of the pressure of playing for United comes from within, because the individual thinks: *This is my big chance. It's got to happen. I was put on earth for this and I've got to take the chance.* If things don't go quite right immediately then you can see them start to lose confidence in themselves and they unravel. The players who had the best impact never allowed their self-confidence to be knocked by events on the pitch. They might go through runs of bad form, but they were able to see that for what it was.

If it was an old stager like one of the Class of '92 boys, they'd been around the block enough times to know that form was transient. If it was a younger lad or a new signing, they just needed to accept that everything wouldn't just catch fire in an instant. Rather than panic about what was going wrong there and then, they needed to recognise that they were in the midst of a process. Don't panic and try to do too much.

If a striker wasn't hitting the target, you'd often see them drifting out of position so that they could get more of the ball. This was a means of rebuilding confidence because if he picked the ball up on the byline and found a team-mate with a pass, he'd be involved in play, he'd be contributing to the team and he wouldn't be under pressure to score from the byline. In fact, what he should have done was remained patient, stayed in position and allowed the chances to come. The biggest confidence boost a striker could have would be to score a goal, so his time was infinitely better spent in the box missing chances than outside the box avoiding them, because sooner or later that goal would come and it would work wonders for his confidence.

All the very best players I worked with had unshakeable confidence in their own abilities and very, very rarely felt pressure as a result. It was always sad to see good, talented people fall foul of their own insecurities, which happened quite regularly in an environment where performing well and winning trophies was the base standard, but self-belief in what you're doing is absolutely paramount to success in life, not just at United.

We brought in a lot of players during my time at the club and, naturally, not everyone enjoyed an amazing career at United. There were a few who simply weren't good enough to cope with the high standards, and that quickly became clear on the training pitch. The saddest cases were those like Diego, who had such obvious ability but just couldn't translate that into consistent performances in the first team.

Two others always spring to mind: Juan Sebastian Veron, who was a sensational talent but always carried an air of frustration with him, and Anderson, who was simply lazy. Seba was a terrific lad who worked hard but, I think, struggled with the language barrier. Ando was an incredibly popular character around the place, beloved by everyone – especially the gaffer – but he was so lazy in training and had real issues with his nutrition. He very quickly lost his fitness and when that happens at the highest level, it's very difficult to get back.

He could point to the winners' medals he amassed – within 18 months of joining the club he was a world, European and English champion – but I'm sure I'm not alone in feeling that he could have gone much further. I had a stick in my gym and more than once I (semi-jokingly) asked Sir Alex if I could hit Ando with it. He said no at the time, but after a while he eventually came in and said: "Give me that stick, I want to hit him." Anderson was more than capable of becoming a really top player, he just chose not to put in the work, so it's hard to have too much sympathy for him.

With a lad like Diego, who conversely worked so hard, I was very pleased for him to go to Spain and thrive away from Old Trafford. Not least because I was no longer at risk of being struck by an errant arrow.

CHAPTER 21

Everybody Hurts

"In my time at United, Ole went through probably the biggest, most sustained course of rehab I've ever seen in football. He went through so many bad times."

It sounds borderline sick, I suppose, but professionally I always relish getting to work with injured players.

I recognise that these periods were, by definition, among the worst experiences that these people go through during their careers, but my enjoyment – for want of a better word – of those situations wasn't some ghoulish thrill of seeing athletes at a low ebb. It was basically my time to shine. An injured player required lots of time and personal attention, which made rehab the period when I could learn the most and, as such, be the most effective I could be in terms of helping them.

When a player is injured, they firstly have to do their physio work to manage their injury recovery, then the rehab is gaining momentum for actually hitting the ground running and getting back in the team. Once a player is rehabbed into a position where they can start working on strength, you can then start doing speed work, then power, then endurance capacity. The biggest and most important aspect is to strengthen the whole system. Not the leg muscles or upper body or mid-section; it's about the heart, lungs and circulatory system because that's what feeds the legs and other body parts.

You might start training on a bike or a cross trainer with no impact but, after you've had a break from your sport, your breathing's not as efficient, so when you start doing cardio work, you have to build up your endurance again. Then you start adding in some deadlifts, chin-ups, mid-section or core work. All these processes during rehab then start activating the heart, lungs and circulatory system. They're all a necessary part of the process.

It's arduous work and it sounds so strange, but those situations provided some real career highlights, simply because you learn so much. That's where true knowledge comes from, through actually working with somebody and helping them reach a point where they're able to go out and do what they want to do.

The deepest education isn't working with the lads in the sense of doing ordinary conditioning training, it's when you go from rehab into conditioning into performance training that's up and above what you normally do, because you have to hit the ground running when you come back from an injury, and so you've got to do little things that hopefully don't cause another injury. You've got to be absolutely meticulous and these players have to trust that you can get their career restarted again as soon as possible.

Obviously I had my early experiences of getting Roy Keane back into action, but probably the most memorable example of the power of rehab during my start to life at United was with Nicky Butt. He missed much of the end of the 2001/02 season with a knee injury and there was doubt over his future at the club, with Roy and Scholesy established regulars and Seba Veron on board. Nicky and I worked together to get him to a new physical peak, which coincided with him making the cut for the 2002 World Cup in Japan.

England went as far as the quarter-finals and lost to Brazil, but Pele highlighted Butty as his player of the tournament, and before long he was given a new contract by Sir Alex, so his situation dramatically improved in those few months. Butty turned things around with his hard work, but he was also very public and very generous in the credit he gave me. When you hear that, it reinforces your belief in your methods.

Getting the chance to implement them with a player over a sustained period of time was a huge professional privilege, but those situations also allowed me to forge some real personal bonds.

Take Ole Gunnar Solskjaer, for example.

In my time at United, Ole went through probably the biggest, most sustained course of rehab I've ever seen in football. He went through so many bad times. As everybody knows, Ole is a fantastic guy, a true gentleman, but he also has unbelievable grit and work ethic. I saw it in action during endless hours in the gym. We worked together a hell of a lot. His knee was a mess and he hardly played for three seasons between 2003 and 2006. He'd get so far into the process and then break down, or another complication would arise. After he got back to a level where he could play 90 minutes for the Reserves, he had his cheekbone broken and that meant more time on the sidelines.

Everything that could go wrong did go wrong for Ole. He went through hell. He had a hole in his kneecap and they had to take some bone out of another part of his body, mash it up and inject it into his knee. He wore a machine to bed for months on end which ensured the circulation in his knee continued at an optimal level. He tried anything and everything and he never once complained. He must have been screaming inside, but that frustration never surfaced or compromised his relentless determination to get back onto the pitch.

He tried all kinds of different training methods and I was there alongside him, every single day. He made each session a joy because he was fascinating. In physical terms, he didn't necessarily look like the most athletic in the squad, but he set a gym record when it came to the cardiovascular equipment – treadmill, bike, cross-trainer and so on – where he got to level 20 on every bit of machinery for 10 minutes. Nobody else ever touched those numbers. Nobody. He was pretty strong on the weights, too. He came from wrestling stock – his dad was the Norwegian champion for a number of years – but I don't think Ole had wrestled that much. He preferred boxing and was very decent. Even though he'd rather have been out on the training pitch, he just adopted an incredibly positive mindset to being stuck in the gym.

During rehab, you really get to appreciate little details about individuals. Most of the players were constantly thinking: *I should be on the bloody pitch*, but not Ole. Even during the spells in his career when he was fully fit but not regularly starting, he always thought he was so lucky to have the chance to be at United. No matter what happened, even during the lowest moments of his rehab, he was always proud to be there.

Of course, he wanted to start every game, but if he didn't then he was there, ready. His attitude was absolutely fantastic and that's why the gaffer had a lot of time for him.

It helped that when he did play, he always made a difference to the team's fortunes. It's reductive to label him the best substitute in United's history, because he was also exceptional when he started games, but he was able to capitalise despite only having short periods of involvement because of his powers of observation.

He opened up so many possibilities for the team to win, whether he was on the pitch for 15 minutes or the whole game, and I always believed that was because he sat there and observed the opposition players. Not many do that. Ole was watching the players he would be playing against when he came on, looking for faults, minor injuries or anything that could be exploited. He was phenomenal in that way.

I'll give you an example. As I mentioned with Ruud van Nistelrooy, one of the hardest things to do in football is to say you're going to do something and then do it. It's risky business. But those who could do it always stood out to me, and Ole was another. After a couple of very fleeting cameos which had proven to be false dawns, he made his long-awaited return to the first team squad at the start of 2006/07. He needed to be carefully managed, even though he was back scoring again, so the gaffer was very cautious about Ole's usage.

Around November 2006 he had a little break but was promised some playing time over Christmas. As players do in that situation, he started looking ahead through the fixture list. When he saw that United had been drawn against Aston Villa in the FA Cup third round, and thus had three meetings with them in three weeks, he virtually began salivating. He said to me: "Gabor Kiraly [the Villa goalkeeper] has a fault which I can exploit. He has his legs too wide and you have to hit it right bang in the centre because the way he holds his hands, he's vulnerable to the ball going straight through his hands, through his legs and into the back of the net."

We talked about it, had a laugh and joke about it and I said: "Yeah, you've got to prove yourself now because you've mentioned it. You've got to get in a position where you can do that, and then do it."

He did it, of course.

He didn't play in the first league meeting, but he came on for the final few minutes of the FA Cup tie. That's all he needed. Wayne Rooney put Ole clear in the penalty area at an unforgiving angle, but he just put his head down and drilled it absolutely dead centre, through Kiraly's hands, between his legs and into the net. He won the tie in injury-time and everything had happened exactly as he said it would. Over the years that followed, I would show that clip to young lads and explain the back story to the goal, just to underline the benefits of being studious and observant at all times.

* * *

I loved Ole – still do – as is the case with probably my best mate at the club: Alan Smith.

What a character he was. I actually think that I might have crossed paths with Alan in his much younger days, long before we worked together. He always spoke about his parents, who he adored, and he told me that he used to go to Butlin's in Skegness all the time because his mum and dad had a caravan there. We also spent a lot of summers there as a family, and I'm sure I recall this little cheeky blonde lad playing football with our Michael.

Whether that was him or not, Michael and I did end up going on holiday with Alan after he'd joined United. We were at a week of conferences in Washington, he was in Florida and he told us to come over and join him. We did, and what stood out to me there, seeing him in a totally non-athletic setting, was the aura he had.

On the field, he was a snarling, ferocious player, a true hard nut, but off it he had a genuinely sweet personality. People gravitate towards him, especially women. I've never seen anything like it. Yes, he's a good-looking lad, he styled his hair, wore nice clothes and all the rest, but I've never seen a guy cause such a stir among women. Remember that, being in America, he was anonymous as a footballer.

We'd be walking down the street and, after a while, I noticed swathes of women just saying to each other: "Wow, look at that guy," and almost throwing themselves at him. I'd spent time with David Beckham and some obviously good-looking footballers, but I'd never in my life seen anybody with an aura like Alan's. Perhaps it was because I was there, making him look even better. Hold on... maybe that's why he invited me!

The majority of our time together was spent in the gym, naturally, and we'd always spend a lot of time talking when we went on pre-season tours to Asia, China, Africa and so on. He loved hearing stories, you see. He also loved the music his dad used to listen to. You can tell a lot about a player from the music they like. Put on songs from certain eras and if they start singing along to it, you know that, more often than not, they've heard it through their parents.

I always remember on the pre-season tour of Korea, Alan said, "Listen to this song, it's brilliant," and, as pathetic as it must have looked, there we were sharing a headphone each, and the song was *Hallelujah* by Leonard Cohen. "It is brilliant," I said, "but do you know the words behind it? The story of King David?"

"Who the fuck's King David?"

So, I told him the story of King David and gave the song a little more back story. Alan loved hearing tales like that, which became a very useful tool when he required lengthy rehab in early 2006.

He came on as a substitute in an FA Cup tie at Anfield, blocked a free-kick from John Arne Riise with his foot planted in the turf and he suffered a broken leg and dislocated ankle. The pictures were horrific, with his leg pointing one way and his ankle pointing the other. He went straight to hospital for surgery, everything was reset and, before long, he was champing at the bit to get his rehab work started.

We'd train all the time and, as you'd expect, he gave it absolutely everything. He got really powerful. He suffered the injury in mid-February 2006, started rehab a few weeks later and I ended up not making any plans for the summer so that I could come into Carrington every single day and work with him.

We also had company for a few weeks. Wayne Rooney suffered a broken metatarsal for the second time, right at the end of the Premier League season, six weeks before the 2006 World Cup in Germany. That was his first World Cup and he was absolutely determined to be there so, from a personal perspective, that summer was unforgettable for me. We had some great weather, so most days we set up a gym outside in the sunshine and we'd ride around on bikes to help both lads' joint mobility.

That period was the best Wayne ever gave me in the gym. He was unbelievable.

One particular day stood out to me because some of the younger lads reported back early for pre-season training, so I was testing them all to see their maximum reps of press-ups and chin-ups, among other exercises. These boys trained regularly and were good, powerful lads. I got each of them to do their maximum press-ups, and Wayne just watched them, then followed them and beat the highest score by one. When it came to maximum chin-ups – and I never saw him do any in the gym but I knew they did them all the time – he did the same again: beat the highest score by one. Just to show them who the king of the castle was. He loved showing everyone who was top dog.

The media's obsession with Wayne meant that there was a ludicrous amount of press coverage of his race to be fit for the World Cup. Personally speaking, I've never had such a high-profile, high-pressure case to deal with. It was a very specific job with a very tight deadline but he ended up making it over to Germany. Then, as sod's law dictates, Wayne tore his groin in a training session after his first appearance at the tournament, which undid all the good work he'd done and totally compromised his ability to make a positive impact for England.

Alan, meanwhile, was in a much longer process. He kept at it and managed to get back to the first team seven months later, but he did go on to have a lot of trouble with minor injuries which would be in different areas, but still related to that original trauma, for my money. Personally speaking, I couldn't categorise his initial surgery as 100 percent successful. As I watched him work his way back down the path to fitness, I could tell Alan's movement patterns weren't as good as they were before the injury. As both a coach and a friend, I was absolutely thrilled for him when he did come back – and especially when he scored a massive goal in the Champions League quarter-final thrashing of Roma – but I found it hard to watch him struggle during those times.

You can have a serious injury and come back fully. Roy Keane came back bloody stronger from an ACL injury, but he had everything right. His process went through the correct procedures to make sure everything was absolutely right, but with Alan, I don't feel like that happened. I'm not a surgeon or a podiatrist, but I never felt he walked, ran, or played the ball the same way again after that operation. I was on the medical team but I was a coach rather than a physio or a doctor. If I could've had an opinion on a medical matter like that, I'd have said that it needed to be re-checked and done right because it wasn't quite there.

Alan left in the summer of 2007 and I was so sad to see him go on any terms, never mind having not fully recovered from such a savage injury. It always devastated me to see players' careers being so impacted by injury.

Unfortunately, it also happened to Owen Hargreaves, another lovely lad who joined a few weeks before Alan left. There was always a lot of internal debate swirling around Owen, virtually from when he first joined because he was just coming back from a broken leg. He still managed to play and contribute hugely during his first season, even though he was undoubtedly playing through the pain barrier because of tendinitis in both knees. We won the Premier League and Champions League, and he played a major part in both. After that, however, Owen needed help and saw a specialist he knew, who pointed out that his knees were both so full of scar tissue that conventional approaches would be no use if he really wanted to fix them.

There was subsequently a lot of public disagreement over what went wrong with Owen, because he spent virtually three full seasons on the sidelines before leaving at the end of his contract in 2011. Personally, I think that fallout underlines the problem: a lack of agreement between all parties. There's absolutely no question over the ability of United's medical staff, physios or the specialists that were consulted; nor is there any doubt that Owen did everything he could to get back, or that Sir Alex was patient in his hopes to have the player available.

Having had Owen come to me a number of times in the gym during his time out, specifically to talk about the situation and vent his concerns about the process, I had the sense that there wasn't one single path to recovery agreed upon by those involved. Speaking as an onlooker, I'm not convinced that Owen had a clear course of action which he could believe in and act upon. If he had, I honestly believe he could have overcome his issues. That's just my opinion, not fact, and I'm sure if everybody involved were to sit down and discuss what happened, they still wouldn't agree.

What I do know for certain is that I was with Owen doing all his work in the gym and he was working his bollocks off in all the different ways that different people were saying, but none of it was working. He wanted to play for United for another four or five years, not leave after four years having played one season. He committed himself totally to getting himself back physically fit, but the problems in his knees were affecting the way that he felt not about himself, but about what he was being told.

It was a tragic series of events, and one of the saddest aspects was speculation over Owen's mentality. For my part, I'll repeat myself: that lad gave everything he had to become injury-free and showed extraordinary resilience to do so, despite three years of dead ends. He showed ridiculous levels of grit and determination to put himself through such an exacting process. Most people would have given up, but Owen never did.

Labels do get thrown around, unfortunately. If a player is frequently absent through injury, their desire to come back is questioned in some circles and they're cast as mentally weak. It's never the case. It takes an amazing amount of fortitude to forge a career as a professional footballer, with the huge physical and psychological burden of being an elite athlete under constant scrutiny.

* * *

Louis Saha was another example of a player miscast by some. That man was phenomenal in the gym, one of the most incredible physical specimens I've ever come across – not to mention that he was a tremendously affable guy and a stupendously talented striker – but he had unbelievable misfortune with injuries.

Louis worked so hard to overcome the issues which tended to affect his knees, but just couldn't seem to crack it. When he played, he was often unstoppable, but he was never able to really build enough momentum to realise his potential. His issues actually led to a redevelopment at Carrington, based on a theory I had. I was studying sleep at the time and, during one of his periods of rehab, we talked about his rest patterns. It turned out that he didn't sleep enough and when he did, it wasn't of sufficient quality.

He'd come into Carrington unable to concentrate at full capacity and function to the best of his abilities. Moreover, since sleep is a crucial part of the body's recovery process, he didn't get the optimal opportunity to repair and recuperate when he was injured. For me, that comprised a big part of his problem.

As a result of that conversation and the issues that Louis suffered, we ended up having beds installed at Carrington with adjustable mattresses so that players could get some extra rest at the training ground if required. Forget being a footballer; as a human, you need appropriate sleep in order to live properly and effectively, and having the best bed you can afford is one of the most important things you can do. Sleep issues were massive for different players down the years, and that's something we worked to correct as we learnt more about it.

As a coach, you're always looking into new means of injury prevention and treatment in the hope that you can help ensure that players are fit and available to do their jobs. As much as I do relish the challenge of getting them back on track when things go wrong, it would always be my preference to never see athletes having to experience such low periods.

CHAPTER 22

The Eyes Have It

"What intrigued me about Scholesy was that when it came to training and matches, he was untouchable. He might not have been able to get near other players in gym work, but nobody could get anywhere near him out on the pitch."

Taking off my coach's hat and speaking purely as a Manchester United supporter, I did have a favourite player in the squad, and I had done long before I started working at Carrington.

Paul Scholes.

Putting my coach's hat back on, I can tell you that had absolutely nothing to do with his athleticism. The obvious way to impress me in the gym was with physical acumen and fierce determination.

There were players I worked with who, as well as being incredible footballers, were also sensational athletes who probably could have competed to a decent standard in other sports on account of their sheer athleticism. Roy Keane, as I've said, could have boxed, the Neville brothers both played cricket to county standard, and there were countless young lads who might have made a career for themselves in sprinting. Some of the goalkeepers were especially adept at basketball and I've witnessed some mind-blowing games of table tennis and badminton among professional footballers down the years.

As I'd seen with my own kids, Michael and Steven, a physical edge can make a big difference in football, especially in the younger ranks. The vast majority of footballers are among the outstanding physical specimens among their peers from a very early age. They're often fitter, stronger and faster as well as having better ball skills. There are outliers – Lionel Messi, Andres Iniesta and Xavi did ok at Barcelona without being mountainous, for instance – but, for the most part, you can count on most top-level professional footballers being top-level athletes in general.

Scholesy was another exception. In the time I worked with him at the gym, it quickly became very clear that he wasn't very strong, he wasn't very fast and he wasn't very flexible. On top of that, he had a history of getting quite ill; he struggled with asthma as a kid and he developed an eye problem which briefly threatened his career in his 30s. He loved boxing but wasn't of the same level as Roy or Wes, for instance. He had these incredible frailties which meant that he was nowhere near the top bracket of the athletes at United. Basically, he was in the bottom bracket.

You could never categorise Scholesy as the runt or the wimp of the group, however, because he was an extremely hard man inside. He was fearless. He'd take on the devil himself if he had to. Maybe I identified with that spirit as a fellow little guy, but I always liked him despite the fact that his performances in the gym weren't up to the collective standard. What intrigued me about him was that when it came to training and matches, he was untouchable. He might not have been able to get near other players in gym work, but nobody could get anywhere near him out on the pitch. Despite scoring so low on the physical scale, he was always able to function so highly, and I had to find out why. I became fascinated by him.

At times during my first few months at Carrington, I would literally wander out onto the training pitch and spend entire sessions watching just him, just to figure out what set him apart. I'd wonder: *What is it that he does? Why is he so effective?* After a while, I put my finger on it.

He has a forcefield.

For all the time spent in my younger days obsessing over superheroes in comics, I should have seen his superpower sooner. He always had so much time on the ball, had so much space around him and was hardly ever dispossessed, simply because nobody could get close to him. Because he wasn't quick, because he wasn't strong, Scholesy's method of coping was to build this circle of control around him. He mastered that radius of maybe five to ten yards and took it with him all over the pitch.

The key to having this forcefield was his brain. The way he saw events around him and processed them, I firmly believe, was different to the brain functions of virtually every other player. Scholesy was basically able to see everything around him, the full 360 degrees, because he was constantly scanning everywhere on the pitch, near and far. The term 'head on a swivel' could easily have been based on watching Paul Scholes play football.

His mind was continually painting a picture of what was around him and updating it more frequently than the other players on the pitch. In the same way that the best snooker players are thinking a few shots ahead, or the greatest chess champions have mapped out a long sequence of upcoming moves, Scholesy was able to foresee events around him and act accordingly based on what was likely to happen. He was very much ahead of the game.

I was always on the lookout for new equipment to use which could help give players the edge, and one of the best I introduced at United was the Neurotracker, a cognitive training system whereby users would don 3D glasses and track multiple objects as they moved. The better and faster your cognition, the higher your score would be. As it happened, the one-off, all-time high score at United was taken by Ji-sung Park, but if you averaged out the players' scores over multiple sessions, Scholesy was consistently far and away ahead of the rest.

His vision was crucial, which is why it was so worrying when he suffered that eye injury towards the end of his career. Scholesy built his ability because he understood the game completely – he was always watching football. When the ball came to him, he was able to control it without touching it. The ball would be coming towards him, and his movement was such that he wouldn't be touching it, but he would be ensuring that other players couldn't get anywhere near it either. That's why I refer to it as a forcefield.

When you think about his high-level brain cognition, it won't surprise you to learn where Scholesy was top dog in the gym. He wasn't the squad's best boxer, but I used another reaction-testing exercise involving mitts and different coloured cones in a very, very small area. The athlete has to punch or kick the pads and touch the cones depending on the colour I shout, and we're circling around as we do it.

Scholesy was the best at that. He was outstanding. In that central position he could see everything around him.

He knew where the cones were, so when he spun around he wasn't only seeing what was in front of him, he knew what was behind him. That's why central midfield and playing in the middle of the pitch worked for him. All the play came through him, and he was able to know everything that was happening or was about to happen around him. All because of his lack. He knew: *I can't sprint 20 metres faster than this player, I can't be as strong as that player, so what I have to be is the master of this small area. I'll be fast and strong in here. Nobody can touch me.*

He carried that forcefield around the pitch with him to devastating effect for almost two decades in United's first team. The key to the unbelievable career Scholesy had, with all those goals, assists and trophies, was his brain. Always seeing, thinking, imagining. You can't always see everything, but he's got a great vision of what's going on and great imagination of what's out of his line of sight. Yes, his skills with the ball were fantastic. His control, movement, laying off, shooting and passing were all top drawer, but the genius behind the man was his ability to manufacture time and space in which to use those ball skills most effectively.

People often referred to him as a magician, and there was something in that because of his sleight of foot. The magician always knows more than those in the audience and those in the show, and that was the case with Scholesy. His superior brain function meant he usually knew more than everyone else on the pitch.

It also made him a dangerous man around Carrington.

As everyone always says, he was a bugger for picking people

off with balls from long range. He got me a few times. You'd be stood there by the side of the training pitch watching something else, or mid-conversation with someone, and suddenly you'd feel this thud, your head would be spinning and Scholesy would be stood 50 yards away laughing his head off.

He got the gaffer a few times too. You were soon conditioned to be on your toes and have your wits about you. You had to treat it like you were going out to war because you were always in Scholesy's crosshairs. Absolute shitbag, that boy.

* * *

I love him to bits, mind. He spent a lot of time with me in the gym and we had a lot of long chats. While he never did much to court publicity during his playing career and swerved as many media commitments as he could, he was a good talker behind the scenes. One conversation which still stands out in my memory came shortly after Euro 2004.

He turned up one day in pre-season and we were chatting about the tournament. England had reached the quarter-finals and, after we'd covered that off, Scholesy just casually said in passing: "I fucking hate playing for England."

"What??" I was dumbfounded.

"I hate playing for England. I love football, I love coming here, but I hate going away with England. I'd just rather be at home with the kids. You go away, you're sat about doing nothing and I hate it. I've never enjoyed playing for England, not one bit."

"What the bleeding hell do you go for, then?"

"Because you've got to go, it's England."

"Have you?"

"Of course I have. Everybody tells me I have to."

"Who told you that you had to play football when you were a kid?"

"Nobody."

"Oh, so you made your own mind up then?"

"Yeah, I just wanted to play, so I played."

"Who told you to play for Man United?"

"Well, they came and asked me and I said yeah."

"So you wanted to come and play for United. You started playing football because you wanted to, you came to United because you wanted to, you signed a contract and took a wage because you wanted to. Now, you're being asked to do something you don't want to do. Why should you do it? You have the right to say no. No matter what anybody is saying to you, Paul, if you don't want to do it then you should not be doing it. It's bad for you, your family and your team because you'll never play for England like you do for United because you don't want to be there."

He never came back to me about that again. He just stopped playing. I'm not saying it's anything to do with what I said because he would obviously have had conversations with his family and friends about it too, but within a month, he had retired from international football.

Around 18 months later, he had a nasty shock when he started suffering with blurred vision during a game and, when it didn't go away, it was discovered that he had a blocked vein behind his right eye which was causing bleeding. Given the unusual nature of the injury, plus the fact that he was under instructions to rest as much as possible, getting Scholesy through that period of rehab work was a finely-tuned process.

Gail Stephenson, our vision scientist, had a very big part to play and beyond that we all did our bit to make sure he had the best possible rehab while also staying fit. Physios very often don't get looked at, but the set of physios we had at United during my time at the club – Rob Swire, Neil Hough, John Davin and Richard Merron – were brilliant. Marvellous professionals and tremendous lads. They were very understanding with me because I was constantly trying new things – not just with Scholesy then but with all of them, all the time – and they went along with that as far as they could before explaining things from their point of view. We had a really healthy, respectful relationship where we always put the players' wellbeing first.

With Scholesy, boxing was key to his recovery. We did a hell of a lot of speed-reaction work, focus mitts and so on. We'd do it at Carrington and Olympic in the evening or at weekends. If I wasn't available, he'd box with Steven or Michael. The aim was for him to have moving targets all the time, keep his awareness up, keep his head up. He had to be able to move quickly, side to side, forwards to backwards, while being able to see everything possible.

Thankfully, he was starting off from an incredible base. His visual acuity was impeccable, his understanding of speed and movement second to none. So, with all the hard work he put into training his vision, he came back the following season and was quickly playing some of the best football of his career.

Nobody should have been shocked. Some kids are born to be athletes. Paul Scholes was born to be a footballer.

CHAPTER 23

Foundations

"Edwin van der Sar simply said,
'Little man with a big mouth,' and he just
stared at me, then walked out!"

Amongst all the transfer business Sir Alex Ferguson carried out during his time at United, Edwin van der Sar must rank as one of the very best signings he made.

Replacing Peter Schmeichel had been handled badly, hence the sheer volume of goalkeepers I'd worked with during my time at the club. By the time Edwin arrived in 2005, I'd already spent time training Mark Bosnich, Raimond van der Gouw, Fabien Barthez, Tim Howard and Roy Carroll, who all had spells as the first-choice goalkeeper. The gaffer was an expert at rotating his players and keeping everyone sharp and happy, but having revolving personnel in that position was not helping the team.

When Edwin became available to sign from Fulham in the summer of 2005, Ruud van Nistelrooy alerted the gaffer and said that he would be the man to bring stability to the position, while also providing a great presence in the dressing room. Even though he was 34 at the time, he was seen as the ideal last line behind the defence. He was vastly experienced, extremely calm in his style of play, a great organiser and excellent with the ball at his feet, having come through the Ajax school of total football. He was also in extremely good shape – although it took me a while to win him over.

On his first day, Edwin came into the gym with Ruud while I was just coaching the lads as normal. I let on, he didn't say too much. After a little while of barking at everyone, I asked him what he thought of what was going on. Nothing inflammatory, just small talk, and he simply said: "Little man with a big mouth," and he just stared at me, then walked out!

Oh shit, good start, I thought. *Big new signing, experienced international, Champions League winner. Thinks I'm a dickhead.*

I am quite thick skinned. If somebody says something to me like that, it doesn't stop me doing what I'm doing. I'd had kids pissing about in schools, in various sessions down the years, and I'd learnt to keep my calm in the face of cheeky little bastards. In this case, in light of a cheeky big bastard taking the piss, I just carried on training the group.

A couple of days later, I was in the Carrington car park, walking up to my little BMW compact, which was parked next to Edwin's huge Mercedes-Benz. As I got to mine, he was stood next to his, towering over everything, and he just smiled and went: "Oh, little man with a little car!"

All I could say was: "You're a big man with a big car, I can see that. But I'll tell you something: there's one thing about me that's really big."

My intonation was quite clear. I'd heard enough footballers and other athletes bragging about their manhood to know the kind of topics they liked to go on about.

He smiled again. "Oh, what's that then?"

185

"It's my heart."

My tone changed from faux-bragging to straight-faced. I wanted him to take me seriously.

He said: "I know. I've been speaking to Ruud and I've been watching what you do. I'll come in and see you before the end of the week so that I can start my training with you." To my surprise, he added: "Also, I want you to train Annemarie, my partner."

I certainly hadn't seen that coming but, within long, we were firm pals around the place. By that stage in his career, he knew what he needed from the gym and I was able to help provide it.

Edwin's arrival turned out to be crucial to the team's ambitions. His communication skills were the best I've seen in a goalkeeper, to the point that he dramatically reduced the amount of shots the team was facing. A lot of goalkeepers love making spectacular saves, but the fundamental aim of the job is to keep the ball out of the net, and Edwin's approach was always to prevent a shooting situation from ever arising, rather than relish the chance to make a save.

I think Edwin knitted everything together, and to me it was the fact that he didn't just see himself as a goalkeeper diving around the goal to make a save; he was always thinking about our attacking play and his ability to play a part in that. He wanted to keep the ball away from his goal, but if it did come his way and he got hold of it, he always wanted to be launching play forward. He stood out the most, to me, as wanting to get the ball forward quickly and accurately.

Halfway through Edwin's first season at the club, the gaffer also brought in Nemanja Vidic and Patrice Evra, who both added real character and steel to the defence.

They, like Edwin, turned out to be inspired bits of business. It wasn't until their first full season that we saw the best of them, but they both adapted brilliantly to life in the Premier League and went on to become mainstays in the team.

Vidic went on to become the partner to Rio that the gaffer had been looking for. As a player he became beloved by United fans, probably for the same reasons that I loved him to bits. He was absolutely magnificent to work with. Great attitude. He'd spent part of his childhood growing up in a warzone in Serbia, so it's no surprise that he never took any shit from anybody. He was a rock and hard as nails – though, in terms of his physicality, that stemmed from meticulous planning when it came to the gym.

Nemanja didn't do as much training as a lot of the players, but he was very methodical about working each area of his body. You can do too much of one thing and miss something else, so you have to be careful with time management. Vidic was always busy with a lot of things, but if he missed his slot to come and do some work in the gym, he'd just do it the next day and he always made sure the work was done. He timed things very well. He was in the gym every other day, sometimes every third day, depending on how it was going with matches because he made sure he was absolutely match-fit, which I totally appreciate. Like Rooney, he knew how to condition himself for the big day.

While there's the well-established image of Vidic the tough guy and Rio the cultured guy, Rio was the one who spent much more time in the gym and he was actually much stronger; he could outdo Nemanja on everything except legs. Rio loved his body, Vidic wasn't bothered about his; he was bothered about being physically fit for games. Rio knew that he had underlying problems in his lower body and didn't want to overdo his legs, but he loved having that shape, size and strength because that made him feel really powerful, and if you're powerful in your mind then you know you're well set. Twin that with the knowledge that you're really good at reading what's going on during the game and you develop a great feeling about yourself.

It wasn't just the fact that he was in the right position that made him so good, it was the fact that he felt so good about himself because he was in such good condition. Rio had a terrific upper body and mid-section, but was very cautious with his lower body, whereas Nemanja had real quality and much more variety about his approach to his training. The two of them were completely different in the gym and on the pitch, but it worked so well for the whole team – not least Edwin.

Having Nemanja and Rio in front of him meant that Edwin always felt really safe. He had one centre-back who'd get stuck in and one who watched everything that was going on and understood the game to such an extent that he could almost always be where he needed to be at the right time. The balance between the two of them was phenomenal. Then he had Gary Neville on the right of him and either Patrice or Gaby Heinze on his left. I called Heinze 'the gladiator' – terrific lad, full of character, full of power, he'd stick his head in anywhere to stop things happening. I loved his bravery. He'd had issues with injury though. Gaby was the supporters' player of the year in 2004/05, his first season, but a serious knee injury decimated his campaign in 2005/06, hence Patrice's arrival as another attempt to nail down the left-back position.

Just as Schmeichel had proven difficult to fully replace, finding the heir to Denis Irwin's throne had been another issue since his departure in 2002. Sometimes the gaffer had used Mikael Silvestre, sometimes Phil Neville, sometimes John O'Shea, but they could all play in other positions and often filled in elsewhere, so left-back wasn't really sorted out until Heinze's arrival. Then, when he got such a serious injury, in came Patrice, who did unbelievably well to recover from a nightmare debut.

He got absolutely trounced in the Manchester derby and was hooked at half-time with us two goals down. The guts and ability he showed to bounce back from that were incredible.

In Gaby's absence, Patrice was able to learn on the job and play his way into form. Vida also laid down roots. Edwin was flawless for most of the season. Ji-sung Park, the other summer arrival, injected enormous vigour and athleticism into the team whenever he played, while also showing total selflessness by taking up whichever position the manager required of him.

All the while, things were coming together. Rooney had been a sensation from the first moment he came into the club, Ronaldo had a really strong end to the campaign and began to consistently deliver on his promise, Giggsy took up a berth in central midfield in the absence of Roy and Alan, and he was a revelation in there alongside Sheasy. The defensive play was strengthening all the time and building a better and better understanding, going forward we carried real menace and unpredictability. The old heads in the squad appeared reinvigorated by what was going on and the youngsters were joining the dots and showing their capabilities. There were issues, of course. Ruud was unsettled, Roy had left a big hole in midfield and there were ongoing injury issues with Scholesy and Alan but, for the main part, you could feel that something was brewing.

By the time we found form in the second half of the season, we were out of the Champions League and FA Cup, while Chelsea were out of sight in the Premier League, but the League Cup provided an opportunity for the team to win a trophy. Having not won anything in 2004/05, the demolition of Wigan in Cardiff was the first taste of silverware for that team. It was by no means the last.

CHAPTER 24

That's Entertainment

"When I look back on my career in coaching, some of the things I saw during that period were the most staggering feats I've ever seen in a gym. It was electric."

If everything was simmering along nicely in the latter half of 2005/06, it came to the boil in the years that followed.

Ahead of the 2006/07 season, I was really sad to see Ruud go, especially so soon after Roy had left the club, but he was ready to leave and it's hard to feel too bad for a player when their next move is to Real Madrid, so I made peace with the situation. The group who remained at the club were developing really well, to the extent that the gaffer decided he only had to add Michael Carrick to the squad. He was only ever going to come in and bolster the group rather than rock the boat, so for the most part everything was very settled as 2006/07 began.

The press had tried to concoct an issue between Wayne and Cristiano after Portugal had knocked England out of the World Cup, but the perfect response was to put that to bed out on the field, which happened on the first day of the season when we obliterated Fulham 5-1. We were four up inside 20 minutes, and both Rooney and Ronaldo had scored.

With the tone and pace set, we were off at a sprint. Chelsea had been out of sight by Christmas in their first two seasons under Jose Mourinho, so the gaffer really wanted to make a strong start to the new season, which is exactly what happened. That ferocity continued throughout the campaign and, by the end of the season, we were champions for the first time since 2002/03. All season long, there was so much energy and enjoyment around our play, which perfectly mirrored the mood at Carrington.

This will sound like me taking credit, which I assure you I'm not, but the heart and soul of that squad, for me, having witnessed it first-hand, existed in the gym.

As much as I loved him and as important a player as he was, Roy's departure, in my mind, liberated the group a little bit.

He had been top dog in the gym since I'd arrived until the moment he left. Roy did have a laugh in there, but he was really serious about his training. That was the main aim with little room for much else, and everybody followed his lead.

There was always an air of mischief within the group, but I think Roy's presence kept a lid on that, for the most part. Occasionally, wrestling bouts would break out. Rio used to throw me all over the gym like a ragdoll. Eric Djemba-Djemba too. He was short but powerful, and he loved being in there, being around where the big players were, and so he would engage too. I ended up wrestling him, wrestling Rooney, I was basically the gym punchbag. I was using the mitts for punching, but then I'd have a wrestle with them and I don't know how the bleeding hell I survived. Until Roy had gone, however, that was really the limit of the high jinks going on within the gym. The other strand to his departure was that Gary Neville stepped up to become captain. Gary was another who liked a laugh but didn't have a high threshold for mucking about. The captaincy was a busy role so, as he disappeared into the demands of that job, that left the other lads with an opening to come and use the gym as a social hub.

I enjoyed every day that I worked at United, but that period became very, very enjoyable.

When I first went in, it was all about training. As far as the players were concerned, they turned up, worked really hard and did everything they needed to do. For me, it was so simple. The easiest gig in the world, really. When I arrived, the players had never had that opportunity to do something different.

All these players had won everything but their light never dimmed; they always wanted more, always wanted new challenges, so they were constantly chasing marginal gains, constantly asking how to be fitter, stronger, faster. The gym gave them the opportunity to become better, so the likes of Gary, Scholesy, Beckham and the others all really wanted to do what we were doing. It took them away from pure football. They had incessantly practised playing football from the moment they'd joined United as kids, so they were absolutely saturated by it. Even though they loved the game, they relished the chance to have something different to do, like boxing or weightlifting.

Much has always been made of the way that Eric Cantona came into United in 1992 and set the standard in training but, having spoken to Roy, who was there, it sounds like the

Class of '92 lads went above and beyond even what Cantona brought to the club. Everyone's heard the stories about Gary practising his throw-ins against a wall at the Cliff for hours, or David taking hundreds of free-kicks aiming to get the ball through a tyre, and they're perfect examples of the dedication on show.

Working with a group with such strong work ethic was unbelievably easy for me because they had so much enthusiasm. It wasn't that I came in and did anything fantastic, I just think that the type of training we did appealed to them. Combinations of different training was what they enjoyed, rather than isolated moves and distractions.

So, from day one, there was a culture of such hard graft in the gym at Carrington. They respected the place. The real messing about was reserved for the dressing room or the massage room. When Roy left and Gary had the added responsibility of the captaincy, there was an opportunity for a touch more creativity in the culture. We'd settled into this mentality of 'we know we're training hard, but now it's about entertainment too' for the players, plus some players entertaining other players.

Cristiano was the man behind it. Then Rio followed. There were other recurring characters. Patrice latched onto Cristiano in the gym. They really got on well together, as did Rio. That's when they began playing football in the gym at the same time they were doing weights. That was circus time. Scholesy was involved too, but he and Patrice were peripheral in comparison to the main pair, who really got it going. The main order of the day was always business – that never, ever changed – but a social culture came to exist which had hard work within it. When I look back on my career in coaching, some of the things I saw during that period were the most staggering feats I've ever seen in a gym. It was electric.

You'd have Cristiano holding two dumbbells and performing a series of lateral raises while juggling a ball with his feet. He'd be performing these moves simultaneously, then he'd volley the ball over to Rio, who was bent over a bench doing single-arm dumbbell rows, and Rio would head the ball back to Cristiano, who would keep juggling. This went on for minutes at a time without the ball touching the floor. Sometimes there would be a third or fourth party getting involved, like Patrice or Scholesy, and they'd get really ambitious and be stationed long distances away from one another.

If somebody messed up then the others would be all up in arms. Sometimes Scholesy would, purely for his own amusement, start smashing balls around the gym – much to the chagrin of some members of staff. Scholesy was always in there, to the point that I brought in a kettle from home and had it in the gym, so that we could have brews together while we chatted, rather than having to keep buggering off to the kitchen.

The whole air of it was sensational to be a part of. The sheer skill levels were unbelievable. Playing football whilst lifting weights. Everything that was happening was reinforcing theories that I was building about splice training, chaos training and brain training. I was seeing that players can do simple exercises building strength, which is the easiest thing of the lot, but then they were doing skill work, but also keeping the intensity too.

The players just loved it. The gym area had become a social hub. You'd find more and more of the lads going swimming after training or going in the jacuzzi, and you could see that they enjoyed having that area virtually to themselves. The canteen was always full of other staff, while the players' lounge was hardly ever used by anybody for anything. I was there in the gym, but only in the background and they knew that I'd let them get away with what they were doing as long as it was underpinned by hard work, which it always was.

The entertainment value was on a different level. In my early days at United, the squad would gather around Roy and Wes while they went through their boxing routines. In the aftermath of Roy's departure and during Cristiano's ascent to the role of main man at the club, they would gather around and watch him and his mates putting on a circus show.

I can't say for certain because I only worked at United, but I'd be very surprised if there were many other gyms in football clubs which had the blend and levels of hard work, skill and enjoyment that we had. What I can say, with absolute certainty, is that I've never been more entertained than during the time I spent sitting and watching some of the world's best footballers combining their art with gym work.

CHAPTER 25

Pride Of All Europe

"'I was absolutely shit, I'm so fucking
disappointed,' Wayne said, before having an
emotional outburst about his performance.
We were sat there at the bar minding our own
business, then suddenly Wayne was crying
with his head on my shoulder."

After regaining the Premier League title in 2006/07, the gaffer wasted no time in taking the next step. Our recruitment drive in the summer of 2007 was a clear power play, with two of the best young talents in Europe – Nani and Anderson – joining established stars Owen Hargreaves and Carlos Tevez in coming through Carrington's front door.

The squad was absolutely buzzing to be champions and to have a slew of top players raising standards even further. It was a masterclass in kicking on when you were already ahead, so the 2007/08 campaign soon set up to be an unforgettable one.

Cristiano's meteoric rise continued and he took most of the

headlines with a ludicrous run of goalscoring, but the whole squad was on top of their game almost all season long. The group had been put together to win the Champions League and no secret was made of that either inside or outside the club. The gaffer had assembled an unbelievably potent blend of players at their peak, young talents coming to the boil and old stagers who were used in brilliantly strategic fashion. Among them were players who were selected too sparingly to be called regulars but too good to be dubbed fringe players, and they all kept at it and did a sensational job whenever and wherever they were called upon.

Throughout the whole season there were so many highlights as we retained the Premier League title and reached the Champions League final against Chelsea, and people often ask me about my memories of being a part of the travelling party in Moscow.

Of course, I remember the headlines from the final itself: Ronaldo's goal, Frank Lampard's equaliser, near misses for both sides, the tension of extra time, Petr Cech saving from Cristiano, John Terry's miss and, finally, Edwin saving from Nicolas Anelka to win the trophy for the third time in our history. I loved the occasion and it's a night I'll always cherish. However, me being me and being deeply psychologically fixated, the story that always comes to mind when people mention Moscow is something that happened at the post-match party.

Everyone was with their partners, friends and families, all sat at their tables. I probably had a place somewhere, but I didn't get involved in all the table business. I was just sat at the bar all night, not because I was a big drinker, just because I felt more comfortable at the bar. I suppose it mirrored me having a desk on my own in the gym, where people could just come and see me if they wanted.

Having gone to extra time and penalties, the game finished after midnight local time, so we were deep into the small hours of the morning when I was sat there at the bar with the head of security, Henry Kirkland, ex-SAS and full of stories, as you'd imagine. We were deep in conversation when Wayne Rooney came over and perched himself next to me.

I asked him if I could buy him a drink. It was a free bar, of course. So he joined us both and we sat there with a glass of champagne each. It appeared to be a fitting scene, given all the hard work everyone had put in all season. On such a glorious night, we were all sat there savouring the success.

Until, after a moment, Wayne piped up: "It was shit, that."

"What do you mean?"

"I was shit."

He'd been taken off during the final, having spent a lot of the game on the wing. He'd been asked to do that more and more during the course of the season as Cristiano began to drift infield. His header in Moscow a few hours earlier was his 42nd goal of the season – the third highest ever by a United player in a single season – and the gaffer had increasingly used him in a central role as his finishing became deadlier. With Tevez also playing centrally, that meant that Wayne, being such a selfless professional, would be asked to station himself out in a wider role, upping his defensive duties and reducing his chances of scoring. He never complained though and always put in a real shift.

"I was absolutely shit, I'm so fucking disappointed," he continued, and he went on to have an emotional outburst about his performance, to the point where he started filling up. Henry and I were sat there at the bar minding our own business, then suddenly Wayne was crying with his head on my shoulder, and he just couldn't believe how the game had gone. He was a huge part of the team and a big part of the success, but he just didn't feel part of the night because he'd been taken off. It really touched him deeply inside and he needed to get that out. I felt so sorry for him.

At the same time, it wasn't lost on me that people had ordinarily come to me in the gym, where I'd been stationed if people wanted to seek me out, and there was Wayne with his head on my shoulder. We'd spoken previously about if he'd just done this or that differently in the gym, he could be top of *FourFourTwo*'s 100 best players in the world list, but he wouldn't.

He wept bitterly, and it felt almost like he came to me because this is what should have been his great time where he'd done the business and become this fantastic player, but instead he was taken off and the headlines went to Cristiano for scoring and Edwin for saving the penalty. Although he'd said that it didn't bother him, things like the *FourFourTwo* list, I think it did.

The best part is that we talked, and this is how you really find people in a deep manner. Although you're not talking all the time, you're still there for them and on a day like that, when he had his family with him, he came to me, had a sip of champagne and burst his belly, telling me how upset and emotionally hurt he was. We had a really good chat before he went back and rejoined the party.

I mostly stationed myself at the bar throughout the party, so I didn't see too many of the players until it got into full swing.

The Champions League trophy was there and everybody was able to have their photo taken with it. I wasn't planning to do it, but then Edwin spotted me at the bar and said: "What are you doing here, you little prick? Get over here and have your pictures done."

Once I'd got there, a lot of the lads came and got me to have photographs taken together. I was probably a bit different to a lot of members of staff in that I made a point of never asking them for autographs on behalf of other people; they knew I was there to do my job and whatever they needed, nothing more besides. In Moscow, they were pulling me up for pictures and that I really, really feel good about, to this day. There are virtually no photographs of me at United doing what I did, but plenty of shots on my wall from the celebrations that night.

As the hero, Edwin was understandably in terrific spirits afterwards, to the point where he once again felt bold enough to start making fun of my size. He actually picked me up and tried to shove me inside the European Cup, in total confidence that I would fit in there! Thankfully a security guard intervened and spared me being folded up and crammed in, and I've got a lovely photo of that moment up on the wall of my office, signed by Edwin alongside a little Dutch comment which translated simply to: 'Little Mick, thanks for your commitment.'

There are a few others. Michael Carrick signed his with a thank-you for finally getting him some arms, then there's me with the European Cup with Giggsy, Patrice, Anderson, Ji-sung Park and John O'Shea. There's even a terribly-lit one of me with Cristiano near the dancefloor, and I'm still staggered that even though he was so in-demand, he found the time to seek out the old geezer from the gym and pose for a picture with him.

But, while it was a great night and I'm so grateful to have had so many of those moments captured and up on my wall, I always come back to Wayne sitting next to me at the bar and pouring his heart out. To hear such agony from a player who had so much potential and wanted to do so well, you really get to find out how deep football is set into these people, how important it is to perform and win.

People like Wayne relish being at their best and winning. It's just like when kids play any game on the streets or a field; they want to do the best they can and get the result that they want. You can see that in these superstar footballers. Even though Wayne was a world-famous, multi-millionaire footballer and now a freshly-crowned European champion, he hadn't played to his full potential in Moscow and he was devastated by that.

In those moments, you truly see what drives these unbelievably talented, hard-working individuals. It's not about the glamour or the money, it's about wanting to be the best that they can be. If it doesn't happen, that's far more important to them than the money or the contract.

CHAPTER 26

Power Struggles

"It's fair to say that I was old school and didn't fit in with the new school."

Everything in life ends at one time or another. That's not the cheeriest thought, but it's a fact.

I knew when I first joined United that I wouldn't be at the club forever. I thought I might get three years in the job, tops, if I came in and did well. In the end, I did 11-and-a-half years, so I certainly don't look back on my time at the club as anything less than an enormous privilege – the greatest professional thrill of my life, as you can imagine.

That doesn't change the fact, however, that when my time at United did come to an end, I harboured a bit of resentment about it for a period of my life, even though I could see it coming a mile off.

As I've said before, one of Sir Alex Ferguson's greatest traits was his proactivity towards anything new in football that could help give his team a competitive edge. United were the first to appoint a power development coach, which was obviously to my benefit. To my detriment, years later the club was among the first to embrace sports science.

That initially manifested when Carlos Queiroz, who had

been assistant manager during the 2002/03 season, left to manage Real Madrid for a season but soon returned to Old Trafford. When he got back, Carlos recommended to the gaffer that he should bring in Valter Di Salvo. Valter was a very animated, very charismatic Italian lad in his early 40s. He had built a good reputation with his coaching at Lazio, and he had joined Madrid at the same time as Carlos in 2003. Though Carlos only had one season as Real manager and returned to Old Trafford the following summer, he had been sufficiently impressed by Valter's work and quickly set about convincing the gaffer that this guy needed to be brought to Old Trafford.

I had no issue at all with Valter when he joined. I had the same mindset as Sir Alex: if somebody was joining the team and could add something that could make any kind of positive difference, then it was good news. We did differ in some aspects of our approaches, of course.

I suppose a neat embodiment of those differences were the types of equipment we liked to use. I was a coach who lived by free weights, Valter preferred resistance machines and he filled the gym with them. Both have their uses and I do have some resistance machines in my lab today. Every morning when I head over to Olympic to start my daily workout, I use a mixture of machines and free weights, but I will always prefer the latter because they ask more of the person using them. If a gymgoer does bicep curls on a machine, for instance, their range of motion is more restricted than with free weights, which place more demands across the entire body. Anyway, I had my ways, Valter had his, but the players responded to us both and I think we worked well together.

As a department, we were performing well and that helped

the team. After a hiccup in 2004/05 when we didn't win anything at all, we won the League Cup in 2005/06 and regained the Premier League title in 2006/07 – and a big part of the latter success was that we began the season at a breathless pace and nobody – not even Chelsea – could keep up with us. The gaffer had built a squad of players made up of just the right blend and, in Moscow, that was rewarded in the ultimate fashion as we were crowned 2007/08 European champions, just days after winning the league once again.

Going into that season, however, we were dealt a shock on the eve of pre-season when it emerged that Real Madrid had come back in for Valter and wanted him to head back to Spain. He didn't feel he could turn them down, so off he went and there was a vacancy to fill in the early weeks of the season.

Having seen Valter's work with the early versions of sports science, Ferguson was sold on the role that it had to play in the future of football. After consulting the grapevine and then coming to me for my opinion, he took my recommendation and moved for Tony Strudwick, who had been making waves in sports science with Blackburn Rovers. I liked Tony as a person but, from day one, it was a clash of styles professionally that was only ever going to end in one way. He was pleasant, I was an obnoxious little shite. He dazzled with his qualifications, whereas I struggled to write my own name. He was the prince of PowerPoint, I was a warty little Luddite. Whichever way you looked at it, Tony was the future, I was a dinosaur.

However, I was also a protected species as long as Cristiano was at the club.

He was the soul of my gym. Everyone always knew where

Cristiano was, and more often than not that would be in the gym. It was a social hub where the main characters congregated, worked hard and entertained the others, and as long as that was happening, I don't think anybody dared rock the boat and risk falling out with them.

Little things had happened which chipped away at my standing. On one occasion Cristiano was training with me and he sent Tony to go and fetch his agent to come into the gym and meet me, which I daresay Tony found quite degrading. I know I would have. So, when Cristiano left to join Real Madrid in the summer of 2009, there were different strands to my dismay. I got on very well with him personally and professionally, so it was deeply saddening to lose that relationship, and the gym definitely suffered once he had gone.

You saw this sudden change almost as soon as he left. Around the same time, Rio had started to get injuries and, in his absence and the absence of anybody stepping up to replace Cristiano as the main character in the gym, the atmosphere was suddenly different.

I was having my issues with the sports scientists and it became a changeover. Without Cristiano there to essentially protect me, this almost iron grip constricted me and I could see what was going on. It didn't take long for everything I was doing to come under attack.

My time at United was going to end soon.

* * *

When I look back now, I retain my stance in power development over sports science – an argument I'll return to later – but I can completely understand how I came to be phased out. Whatever my strengths as a coach, then and now, I would never claim to be hugely organised. I had relationships with every player in the first-team squad and knew what each of them wanted and needed from me. Doing this with 20-30 senior players, many of them on a daily basis, was as time-consuming as it sounds, so I wasn't in the business of hopping on a computer after each session and logging test results or updating individual training programmes.

As far as I'm concerned, the proof of the pudding is in the eating. My job was to provide the appropriate power development for the players I worked with. I could see the results. They could feel the results. For me, having those results quantified as statistics and logged for future reference wasn't as important as the here and now. Are the players fit, robust and strong in a way that allows them to function better for football? If so, then that's all that matters. Whatever has been put in an Excel document has no bearing in comparison to what is being measured by the players themselves.

It's fair to say that I was old school and didn't fit in with the new school.

Within the department, sports science began to gain more of a foothold, more traction, which meant it required more bodies, which gave it further presence and further traction. The writing was on the wall for me and, as I said, I'd already been wondering for a while how I'd managed to last at United for so long. You don't get saddled with the nickname 'Hitler' by going around brownnosing and gladhanding!

To be honest, I knew that I had to go, that I'd been there too long. For a while I'd felt that there was a different purpose for me. I had this thing in my heart telling me I'd been there too long, I was getting too old to hang around and that my life would go onwards and upwards elsewhere, not at United. Certain events just crystallised my thinking.

It did hit me hard when Cristiano left, and something stirred inside me when Trevor Lea, our nutritionist, departed the club. Trevor was a genius in his field and had means of providing optimum nutrition in the most enjoyable way possible, but his approach wasn't in sync with the general direction being taken, so he went very quickly and quietly. It pissed me off, to lose somebody who was so good at their job, so I vowed to myself that when my time came, as I knew it would, I wouldn't be so accepting of it.

Nevertheless, it was a long process with a lot of disagreements along the way. One memorable instance was when sports science as a collective disapproved of the mid-section work I was coaching, citing it as a back injury risk, even though – as the medical staff attested – I'd never had a single instance of it causing a back injury in all my years at the club.

* * *

I'm mindful of being crass by diving too deeply into the ins and outs of my departure, but I like to think that it won't ruffle too many feathers to share the broad circumstances.

So, because sports scientists were so fond of number-crunching as a means of proving their capacity to enact positive change, they built a dossier that showed one of their coaches could make a certain player stronger than I could. It was Oliver Gill, son of the club's chief executive, David Gill. Lovely lad, a decent defender in the youth team. I coached Ollie at David's house a number of times and he was also doing extra training with our Steven at Olympic twice a week to give him a better chance of progressing through the ranks.

That worked and when he got into the Reserves, the strength and conditioning coaches had him deadlifting 120kg within a few months, whereas I'd purposely capped Ollie's load at 70kg. So there it was. Never mind that I'd raised two footballers and two weightlifters who had made it to the world championships; sports science as a department were able to make Ollie 50kg stronger for working with them, which meant I was shite.

That extra 50kg that Ollie could lift is all well and good in a gym, but where does that become useful on the pitch? I don't recall too many instances down the years of players having to lift barbells during a match, nor could I envisage a footballing situation where the ability to lift that extra load would come into play… perhaps a set-piece routine where Ollie would lower himself into a squatting position and allow his team-mates to launch themselves off his quads.

The questions I would ask in that situation are: what has that extra load done to his form, his body, his ability to move around a football pitch?

Nevertheless, the point had been made: strength and conditioning coaches, through the use of sports science, could make Manchester United's footballers stronger than I could. That put them, neatly enough, in a position of power.

Personally, I think they were blinded by numbers. Coaching is an art, not a science. When too much focus is put on the numbers, players can become collateral damage. Zoran Tosic is a player who immediately springs to mind on that front. He arrived midway through 2008/09 on the recommendation of Nemanja Vidic, and it was immediately apparent that he needed to fill out in order to be able to cope with the physical demands of English football. The gaffer provided the very simple remit: "Get him bulked up." Now, from my experience, that meant being done in a football-specific way over a healthy amount of time. Ronaldo was the perfect example of how it should be done, and he was still at the club at the time.

All Zoran had to do was look across the gym and do it like Ronaldo did it; insistently, day on day on day on day over years as he was developing his skills, developing his understanding of the game, developing his body. It takes time, it's a balancing act. You don't start putting mass on a lad who's trying to develop his skill for football. Football is about football skill and being able to play.

Zoran arrived as a very small, but very talented £7million winger. He was 21 and had just been given the biggest chance of his life, so the focus should have been on assimilating him to the squad on a football level. Instead, the focus was put on making him physically ready and he wasn't able to cope with all those demands. He made five substitute appearances in two seasons and then left the club. It pains me to this day when I think about the tragedy of that lad's United career because he never had the help he needed. That's not to say that there was any guarantee of him making it into the team ahead of Nani or Giggsy, even after Ronaldo had gone, but he just never stood a chance.

Zoran was the subject of running arguments between myself and the sports science department, to the point that it began to affect our ability to work together. I was bemoaning that very fact on the day that my time with the first team came to an end, back in May 2010. I don't look back on my life and think there has been too much salacious material that would have constituted tabloid fodder, but surprisingly enough the argument that led to my reassignment within the club did make it into the *News of the World* at the time. So, since it's been out in the public domain before, I think I'm on safe ground to admit that Tony and I had a bit of a scuffle. I won't go into too much detail, but I'll put it into a bit of context.

After training, I was in the hot tub at Carrington chatting with Darren Fletcher. The topic turned to the ongoing loggerheads between myself and sports science, so I started badmouthing them. Little did I know, one of them was listening to the conversation behind a nearby door. He burst out, tackled me on something I'd said, I responded in no uncertain terms and off he scurried.

Shortly afterwards, when I was back in the gym, Tony burst in and berated me for making a member of his staff cry. Fair play to him, he was sticking up for his team. In his position I'd have done the exact same thing. Thing is, I was the only person on my team, so I had to stand up for myself. In that moment, with Tony jabbing his finger at my forehead, I knew my time was up. I also knew that I owed it to myself to go out with a bang, so I grabbed hold of his fingers and threatened to shove them up his arse. Things went from there, we had a bit of a grapple and it went on for maybe a few minutes. Tony and I were the only two people in the gym, so only we know what happened in there.

With it making the pages of the *News of the World*, the gaffer naturally knew about it and he was quick to have a word. "Look, just behave yourself," he said. "We'll be looking at things at the end of the season so don't be falling out with

Tony in the meantime." The gaffer was always very fair, so I would assume he had a similar conversation with Tony, but it was obvious to everyone that the little crack between us had become a moat by this stage.

At the end of the 2009/10 season, I was reassigned to work in the Academy, which was based in a different building on the same complex, maybe 100 metres away. The gaffer said: "You know how you came in here, took control of the gym and everyone loved it? I want you to go and do the same over in the Academy now and help the young lads develop. Go over there and do what you did here."

I was thrilled. My remit was to go over there and install a gym in the same fashion that I had in the first-team building, and I was given carte blanche to carry out as much research as I wanted, wherever I wanted. I suspect that Sir Alex saw it as a win-win: the team would continue moving forward under the new regime, sports science could rest easier without a short-tempered dinosaur berating them to the point of tears, and said dinosaur could go out foraging in the big, wide world. I agreed with him absolutely. Problem was, Brian McClair didn't. Brian was the head of United's Academy and was a strict opponent of gym work.

Following the gaffer's remit, I'd flown to Pittsburgh on a research trip into rehab for kids. Brian bollocked me for not running it by him first, then went on to explain that he'd enjoyed a long and successful career without once setting foot in a gym, and that all any generation of footballer really needed was 10,000 hours of work with a ball at their feet.

So, after spending the 2010/11 season essentially left to my own devices, filling a gym which was never going to be used, I was told by Brian at the end of the campaign that there was no longer a job for me. I could hardly say I was shocked, could I? I'd seen the signposts and I was ready to return to Olympic on a full-time basis and take that forward, so I knew my next move quite a way in advance.

I'd be lying, however, if I didn't admit that I had mixed feelings over leaving United. I'd been a fan my whole life, I'd contributed to a successful chapter in the club's history and I'm not ashamed to admit that for a few years, I carried a lot of bitterness about the way everything had ended.

As much as I was ready for a fresh start, ready to get out there and start making a difference to the lives of anybody who needed my help, there was certainly a part of me that was gutted.

When you walk out that door at Carrington – especially with the way everything had panned out over the previous couple of years – you look back, then look forward again, you can only think one thing.

Shit, there's no turning back.

CHAPTER 27

Brain Drain

"I assumed Darren Fletcher's injury problems stemmed from him being relatively frail and weak for a footballer. I'll never forget the day he proved me wrong."

What is power development?

I always, always get asked this question.

It's very easy to assume that power development, strength and conditioning and sports science are all basically the same thing in different guises: the process of trying to strengthen and improve athletes. In fact, they are vastly different.

I first submitted a power development model to Manchester Schools in 1995, pre-dating both sports science and strength and conditioning. That model has constantly evolved, and never faster than when I arrived at United in 2000, because I was suddenly exposed to the most unbelievable experiential education imaginable.

To that point, the main aspect of my early coaching in football was working with Michael and the school team plus higher-level players representing Tameside Boys. I was obviously always very passionate about watching Michael play and it was hugely enjoyable seeing improvements coming from the little bits that we had worked on together, because they were making him a better, more functional player. He could get to the ball first or get it off an opponent and get it to somebody on his team, whereas he couldn't before, so you build up on those foundations and, over time, those improvements led him to Manchester United.

I'd been used to mainly working with defenders and Michael was the main subject of that. Coming through those doors at Carrington opened a gateway for my own development. The guys I was suddenly working with were thinkers, seers and creators who had been students of the game throughout their lives.

They were seeing what was going on at a much higher level than Michael. The physical edge that he'd built over time was being trumped by the football education these boys had devoured from an early age.

That then prompted me to think in terms of brain training and wonder how we could really understand brain cognition. How could we get some kind of instrument that could tell us if a player's brain cognition or multi-tasking was improving? I woke up in the middle of the night at one stage during my time at United with one phrase thudding around my brain: *rapid cognition, rapid cognition, rapid cognition*. It was the most exciting thought that struck me.

To an extent, I had already been doing that with the lads in Olympic. I used to put out seven different coloured cones, while also using focus mittens and pads, which they'd be kicking and punching. They'd go through one of four combinations – punch or kick my left or right hand – then I'd shout a specific colour cone for them to touch and they'd come back and keep following instructions. This all took place at high speed.

I'd be moving around in different directions, so the target was moving, then they'd have to process the colour I was shouting, then as they sharpened in those tasks I would start asking them questions too. Multiplications, backwards spellings, memory tests… the higher level they got, the harder the questions would be. I was splitting their brains and honing their cognition.

Thankfully, that was great preparation for United. I'd already learnt to train brain cognition and multi-tasking, but the great part for me was that I was able to see what they were doing well or where they were making mistakes in matches, while also listening to Sir Alex and the other coaches as they identified other areas of improvement which I might not have seen. My job was then to bring all that into the gym to understand what would work to fix their problems and accelerate what the lads were doing well.

Over the course of my career, before, during and after United, at the heart of all of my work with power development was the theory that the most important part of the body was the brain. For me, power development is all about the brain. From all my years of working with neuroscience, going on a trip to Montreal University and spending time in their lab with renowned neuroscientist Jocelyn Faubert and his protégé David Tinjust, I'm able to see it from the point of view of the athlete being able to succeed in whatever they're doing. In football, it was always important to break it down to the basic core idea so that the player can understand what they were doing, what was going on in their mind and then, when we spoke about it, they understood why they were doing what they were doing.

The brain is a very complex organ but it contains very simple, layered processes. If you tap into them through different models to see how it all works together, you can see the different layering that goes on in the mind and that's why you know the brain is the powerhouse of the person. It's that which gives energy to everything that goes on in the body. Ultimately, we're looking to harness and hone the power of all the assets and facets of the brain.

Sports science disagrees fundamentally. A sports scientist will, for example, look to measure how fast footballers are over 40 metres. Ok, fine. Player A is faster than Player B on the results chart from those tests, but would you have Player A in the team based on that? He's faster at getting over the distance, but does he see what's going on when he has to decelerate and make a tackle or a pass? There are a whole host of different things that you need to be looking at when you do that.

So, in my power development drills, a player has to accelerate from the starting point to start the timer off, but then when they're through the other timer at the end of the required distance, then they've got to decelerate, get into composure mode (where they bring the body and mind under control) and strike the ball at a target. So, rather than sprint in a straight line between two points, they will sprint that same distance, but factor in their proximity to the ball, their speed in relation to that proximity, then the angle of approach, their footwork in striking the ball and, most importantly, the act of hitting the target.

I always start an acceleration/speed session with a three-metre zone for the initial take-off where the athlete is smashing their feet into the floor for traction. Then, as the stride lengths extend, the whole body takes a different shape, particularly as shifts in arm use begin. At this point the emphasis needs to flow to the visual field, like when a cheetah has selected its prey which, for a footballer, is usually running for the ball. This is ignored within strength and conditioning, where the running is done purely within two points, totally failing to fire up the visual field.

Football is about skill, not just running fast in short bursts. This drill needs to have a visual target for deceleration and composure in order to segue into the skill element which football is all about, and it is also hugely important in helping the athlete to avoid hamstring tears, which is a common occurrence within football. My drills rely on specific deceleration for football, rather than the Nordic leans favoured by sports science, as they totally mix up the brain's ability to select muscle fibres from the muscle groups required to slow down. It's just more dangerous to the players.

At United, I talked to the sports scientists about this very matter. It was not scientific, they said. The gist of their counter-argument was: it's not science, so you can't use it. We need science to make these players better.

I remember shouting: "What do you mean, you can't use it? That's what goes on in the game!"

It just didn't make sense to me. I was explaining what the players needed to perform and, because they couldn't measure it in simple numbers, they wouldn't buy into my explanation of my methods.

I believe this is because the model of thinking within sports science is based on established strength and conditioning concepts of total isolation in singular exercises which simply don't allow for my theory of power development. The idea that getting someone who has being doing, say, 40kg deadlifts, then training them up to do 140kg makes them a stronger footballer is one of the most naïve things I have ever witnessed.

The amount of damage that can be done to players who have to multi-task, and quickly move in different directions with different athletic and skill processes, is vast. All aspects of specific game-related movement have to be carefully fitted together to make sure coherence in the player is maintained. You cannot mix iron and clay and expect a good outcome.

Strength and conditioning as a concept has its roots in American football. Call me a stickler for semantics, but I've never gotten over the name of American football, as compared with English football. American football uses an odd-shaped vessel as their 'ball', but it's not spherical. They also very rarely kick this oddly-shaped object; instead they throw it. It definitely is American, but it definitely isn't football, whereas English football is most definitely an accurate name.

Anyway, the layout in American football is where you have a line of big guys trying to get to the opposing quarterback, whose only job is to pick out somebody to throw the ball to while being protected by another line of big guys. It happens for a few seconds, the play finishes and they have a huddle while the coach comes over and says exactly how they're going to act in the next play. I never saw Sir Alex Ferguson wander over to his team and tell each of them exactly what they were going to do next and where they were going to be!

Another issue has arisen within strength and conditioning because of the adoption of an American sport to base the model on. The naming of activities in England is different to conventions in America. What is referred to as power lifting in strength and conditioning is, in fact, strength lifting. What is known as Olympic lifting in this model is, in fact, power lifting, but this has all been lost in translation. For the hopes of athletes, who wish to specifically play their sport better, to be based on a confused model, is madness as far as I'm concerned. In an industry of marginal gains, think of the athletes who have been failed since this model came in. As coaches, we're here to maximise athletes' potential, not limit it.

For me, it's fundamentally the wrong model upon which to base the coaching of footballers, but it has been in the game for years now and has become a prevalent force therein. You find some sports scientists now taking young footballers, mere kids, and teaching them to lift heavy weights to prove that they are stronger than they were before. It's all well and good being stronger on a chart, but it doesn't make them stronger on the pitch; it means they're more able to lift something up that they weren't able to before. Out on the pitch, the areas that you need strength are just as unique as the areas where you need deceleration and composure. When you're using strength to hold somebody off, you don't need the ability to squat three times your own bodyweight. It's ridiculous.

Look at Darren Fletcher, for example. Going off appearances, Fletch was tall and skinny – over six feet tall but probably weighing 70kg wringing wet. He used to have a lot of injury problems in his early days, including a broken leg at one stage, and I personally assumed that this stemmed at least in part from him being relatively frail and weak for a footballer. I'll never forget the day he proved me wrong.

He'd previously mentioned that he was quite decent at hockey so, one afternoon at Carrington, it spilled over into a game inside the caged artificial pitch. I couldn't get anywhere near him. Not a chance. Regardless of how much strength I had built from years in the gym, in that situation Fletch was stronger than me because he had functional strength. That skinny kid could hold you off for fun with one arm while he was using his stick in the other. That had nothing to do with having massive quads and glutes and shoulders; it was down to his ability to move very rapidly and then he could hold you off with his long arms. He knew exactly how to position and angle himself and make it impossible for you to get around him. That's why he was able to hold his own in the Premier League against the likes of Patrick Vieira, Steven Gerrard and Frank Lampard, who had bigger names and bigger statures, but he gave them as good as he got.

In the era of sports science, Fletch would have been prescribed squats, deadlifts and other static moves to build the numbers he could lift, but would that have translated into the functional strength that he needed to hold off opponents in a congested midfield? Not a chance.

You can't get that sort of information and understanding by going to university or speaking to somebody who's not directly watching what's going on. The experiential learning I enjoyed during my time at United was absolutely priceless; a once-in-a-lifetime education which just couldn't be replicated in a lecture theatre.

* * *

My focus was always on the brain, but it was only as time

wore on and I spent more and more time observing these incredible footballers that I concluded the best means of power development.

The brain uses neurons and axons, which are basically machines that make you do everything you do. There are certain neurons and axons in the brain which make you do a squat, then different ones to make you jump. Now, footballers need to be good at the squatting, but not too good because they don't want to entrench themselves, and they need to be good at jumping, but not too good because they're not jumping all the time, but what they do need to be really good at is the combination of the two, so the ability to shift from one neural pathway to another. It's that explosiveness, that ability to change from one exercise to another. That's the key.

You've got loads of different exercises – accelerate, change direction, decelerate, balance on one leg, hold off an opponent and kick the ball in a specific way – and the most important part within that process is to be able to transfer from one exercise to another.

We use transitional axons in our brains to link all these different exercises together. It's that area that we need to be really, really powerful in: strong in the ability to move from one to another. Not to be able to do 200kg squats. Not to be able to jump two vertical metres. That's what strength and conditioning is entrenched in. Everything is one exercise on its own. Isolated. The abilities of a footballer are never isolated. There are so many things they've got to do almost at the same time.

Everything clicked for me on one day, when a coach came to work with me and paid for a course I was running on power development for footballers. As I was showing him the different types of training methodologies I utilised, he told me he had previously been on a strength and conditioning course, and everything I was showing him was in direct conflict to that course. I was then informed, to a blend of horror and hilarity, that what I was doing sounded like what strength and conditioning coaches referred to as 'the specificity trap'.

Oh my word. That was the moment that I became convinced that sports science had gone too far. All these people with enough qualifications to wallpaper their houses, saying how it should be from a scientific point of view, and they had completely cut the brain out of their calculations and built a robot that was totally unfunctional. They were basically saying that these athletes who can tell us what they need should be ignored and instead be told what they needed by scientists who had crafted the answer to what is required on the field of play. Wow.

To really discover what is needed in the athletic arena, you need to watch what the best do, then copy the resulting actions you have seen, isolate and then move through the different processes to learn how things are done. Once you've figured that out into a sequence, then speed it up, then put it under pressure, then put it in a game. This is basic skills performance, not rocket science and I can say from decade after decade of experience – before and after sports science – that it will produce high-level functional athletes that can play the game and exploit their creativity. It will also produce new abilities in different ways to become more able to create and use and win. End of. Having coached athletes in most sports, I'm absolutely convinced that football is the most intricate sport there is, and the most difficult to learn. Players have to be able to accelerate and run at high speed, decelerate, then go into composure, get into position, to then process the location of a target, then hit that ball into that target while other people are charging at them, while standing on one foot while the other one is doing something incredible.

We don't use our feet to write, feed ourselves or anything intricate like that in everyday life, yet a footballer does their most incredibly dextrous, skilful, subtle deeds with their feet, usually while using one of them to stand on.

This game of unbelievable skill lasts 90 minutes with only one designated break of any length and requires supreme fitness while competing against other supremely fit athletes. It's an absolutely incredible sport, simple as that. Without any disrespect to American football and fans of the sport, it drives me mad that a game of such simplicity is the basis for a huge part of training modern footballers.

That's why, to this day, I can't accept sports science as the best means of development in football. I've seen the results of power development and, while they might not have registered in big numbers on charts, they were – in my opinion – more visible out on the pitch.

That's why, even though my apparently outdated approach had led to my departure from United, I have persisted in developing it ever since I left Carrington.

CHAPTER 28

Old Friends And New Horizons

"I never really imagined that he would come back but, a couple of days after he arrived, Michael got in touch to say that Cristiano had been looking for me at Carrington. What a moment that was for me."

I suppose my life after United really started before I'd left the club.

With the gaffer so open to progress and advancements, I saw the problem between me and sports science developing and growing. At the time, I was still reading about the brain and its role in human behaviour, and one thing that stuck with me was that if you want to change your direction in life, you've got to change a lot of things. Say, for example, you wanted to get out of your dull, boring job, the worst thing you can do is keep getting up every day at the same time and going through the motions of the same routine. It's a repetitive process which drags you deeper and deeper until you become solidified in it, and once that happens then it's very difficult to get out.

The gist of what I was understanding was this: you've got

to change everything if everything's going to change. So, I started driving a different direction to work each day, coming home a different direction, and all the things that had been set: eating times, sleeping times, everything like that, I just ripped them up and did it all differently because I knew that big changes were coming my way. If you're already in the process of changing the way you're thinking and acting, the big change isn't actually a massive happening which shocks you. If you're not ready for it, changes like that can scar you.

I was even changing my methodologies in training because there were increasing restrictions to what I was doing. I didn't have access to everybody. I hardly got to work with the Da Silva twins, for instance, which is a shame because I think I could have helped them with their recurring injury problems. Obviously, nobody was going to tinker with the routines of the established pros, because nobody wanted to upset Paul Scholes or Rio Ferdinand, so I kept working with them.

That was great for me because it continued to open other doors. Rio introduced me to Mahmud Kamani, then-multi-millionaire (and now billionaire) owner of the clothing company Boohoo, and I trained him for a while – even though his busy schedule made it unbelievably tricky to carry out. He just couldn't relate to anybody who was telling him what to do in a fitness sense. Rio told me that I needed to help Mahmud sort himself out or he was going to die young because his weight was out of control. So, I spent a lot of time watching Mahmud work in his office, learning about him from his staff and asking him questions about himself.

When we started training, his phone would be going off constantly. I used that to make one big change to his regime. I set a rule: every time that phone went, he had to answer, get on his exercise bike and start cycling while he talked. If he wasn't prepared to do that, then I would leave; those were my terms. He had to answer and start cycling because he was an emotive character when he talked business, so I wanted him to channel that emotion into driving his heart rate, blood pressure, circulatory system and so on. That alone was the best way for him to make improvements because it gave him a methodology to harness his emotions and use them as fuel. Over a few years of working with him, he lost some weight and greatly improved his health and fitness. The risk of dying a young millionaire went away and he's now a billionaire.

Scholesy, meanwhile, talked about the possibility of opening up a gym – we actually looked at buying Ashton Old Baths when it came up for sale – as did Gary Neville, so there were a few lads who wanted to do bits together even after it became clear that I was on my way out.

In the short term, I had the security of Olympic. To further reinforce my safety net, in 2010 I rented a smaller room on the floor below Olympic at the mill and began training private clients in there. One of the very first was Aaron Cook, who was a 19-year-old taekwondo player at the time. His dad came to see me after reading an article online about my work. Aaron was very highly rated and was already in Great Britain's taekwondo squad, but he didn't rate their coaching set-up and he was looking for someone to train him personally.

I was very interested. Aaron came along, we met, we trained and then, of course, got down to the thorny issue of money. He wanted to know what it was going to cost him to keep working with me. I thought about it and, since I was still being paid for my day job at United – even though there was less and less that I was able to do – I told Aaron I'd train him for nothing. My evenings were free, I was under no financial pressure at the time, I liked him, he had potential, so why not? I trained him for free for a year and didn't start charging until I left United in July 2011.

When that time came, I went to see a solicitor about my contract – all standard stuff within the departure process – and it was actually a former United player-turned-solicitor, Colin Murdock, who went through everything with me. United did right by me and I was happy at the end of the process, no complaints there.

The strange part of all that was that, while I was waiting to go and see Colin, I was sat on a wall in Piccadilly Gardens in the centre of Manchester when my phone rang.

Roy Keane.

He'd finished managing Ipswich a few months earlier, he'd come back home, and he wanted to start training with me again. We'd crossed paths a few times when he'd been at Sunderland with our Michael and I'd been up visiting, so we were still occasionally in touch. He wanted to start up boxing again, so he came to the gym. From that, Nicky Butt came down too. Colin Murdock also sent a few players my way, including Matty Gilks, who was first-choice goalkeeper at Blackpool and worked with me for the next decade.

I didn't have time to miss United, nor did I have any real inclination to think back on what I was missing. It was vital for me that I'd changed my thoughts, because changing your mind changes your heart which, in turn, changes the decisions you make. The process of life post-United was seeing the future before it happened. A door opens, you see a little bit of light and you just follow that opportunity to see what's possible behind the door. Once you've seen that, the light just spreads and you end up following this journey of life just opening up opportunities. What was happening felt fantastic.

People would turn up out of the blue, whether it was someone like Butty or Roy from the past, or a new client who had read or heard something about my work and wanted to see if I could help them. Everything took off to the extent that, in 2014, I moved my little lab out of the mill and to nearby premises next to Ashton Canal.

The reasoning behind that involved the growing client base and, believe it or not, an Alsatian. When I was in my mid-20s, I'd had a dog called Rocky. He'd lived through Olympic's formation and my divorce from Sue and he spent a lot of time going back and forth between the gym and the house. A few years after Rocky died, Shaun had turned 18 and he asked if I could help him pick out a dog and train it. That's always been a string to my bow; I've had a few people bring their dogs to me so that I can train them and it's hard work but I love it. I took Shaun down to the dogs' home in Harpurhey and a little Alsatian pup had been brought in the previous night, having been found abandoned. I wasn't sure, but a member of staff really went to work on my heartstrings and, with Shaun in favour, we ended up having the dog.

We named him Rocky 2. The best friend I've ever had.

He spent all his time with me but, with the gym having so many customers, the decision to move to the new premises was partly down to having a big enough space for Rocky to run around without getting in the way of the athletes. He became the king of the place, and so important to the whole experience of training with me. He would essentially be the front of house, meeting and greeting anybody who arrived on the premises with a lick and a sniff. Didn't matter if it was Roy Keane or some kid who was pitching up for his first training session; Rocky gave them all the same treatment and he was beloved for it. Some people might have been a bit frightened when they first saw him because he was a big dog, but he was so gentle that he became a feature of the lab.

* * *

I spent years after I left United looking for the next Ronaldo. Every time a new young footballer came into the gym, I was sizing them up and seeing if they had what it took to reach superstardom. For a brief time, I actually had hopes that John Guidetti, Manchester City's young Swedish striker, could be that man, but it never materialised despite so much promise shown in our sessions. Another who sticks out in my memory is Johnny Gorman, who played for Northern Ireland at 17. He was at United but went to Wolves because they offered him a better contract, and he never reached his full potential.

Football is an unbelievably hard sport in which to reach the highest level. I've been excited by quite a few young players over the years, but they often bloom like flowers and then wither when the sun goes away. You inevitably forget about most of them because the next age group are coming through. They've got to seize the moment or they're gone forever.

So many young players are sent to me by agencies looking to give their clients the edge. I must have had over 150 players from one agency alone, virtually all of their clients coming from United, City, Liverpool, Everton, Blackburn and Wigan. They come, have a few sessions, tell me how great it's going and vow to be there all the time, but that dries up when the agency stops paying for extra sessions and they've got to pay their own way. The parents often think they've seen enough of the training to replicate it themselves to some degree, but it doesn't work.

Those players, however gifted, don't stick out in my mind. The ones who I remember best are the dedicated ones. Lewis Travis from Blackburn Rovers, Tim Chow who was born in Wigan but plays internationally for Chinese Tapei, Otis Khan – once of United and now at Walsall, Jack O'Connell who helped bring Sheffield United up to the Premier League; these are lads who came week after week for years. Stephen Ireland really impressed me when he came in after a bad first season at Aston Villa and improved to the extent that he was named their Player of the Season a year later.

Footballers were my main clientele, but in those early years after moving to the lab, Aaron was probably my star pupil. His progress had been meteoric. In taekwondo terms, Aaron was technically brilliant when I first started working with him, but he needed to make strides in his power and his mentality. He needed the killer instinct, the emotional force required to kick an opponent in the head and knock him out cold. In his first year of training he took absolutely huge strides forward and became world number one, winning grand prix after grand prix and the 2012 European Championship in Manchester. He was top of his league for five years after we started working together. In that time, his issues with Team GB became so fraught that he actually switched nationality and started representing Isle of Man, so he was delighted to win the 2014 European Championship in their name.

As Aaron's career continued, he again switched national allegiance, this time to Moldova, but he never quite managed to scale the heights he could have reached. Olympic gold was the aim at Rio 2016, but there were issues over his training schedule. He had a specialist taekwondo coach, while I looked after the rest of his training, but there were disparities between our methodologies and the one who paid the price was Aaron, who exited Rio in the preliminary round in what was a huge upset. Nevertheless, we've remained close friends. He retired in 2021 and he still comes to train at the lab. For a long time, he was coming in with his girlfriend, Bianca Walkden – who won a bronze medal in taekwondo at the Rio Olympics, and again at Tokyo 2020, not to mention three world titles – and that made for some incredible sparring sessions. Being two of the world's best taekwondo exponents, romantically involved, but still kicking each other senseless in my lab – I could have sold tickets to that. They've since gone on to open their own taekwondo club at Manchester's Etihad complex, and the pair of them have taken on a lot of my training theories, so I'm very excited to see where they end up.

While we were training for competitions together, Aaron was a huge part of the culture going on in the lab. It was unbelievably busy at times, totally chaotic with clients ranging from golfers to American football players, but, from an elite coaching perspective, it was beyond thrilling.

I was training a girl called Sara Howarth, who ended up working for me. It was a family affair because her mum cut my hair and her dad was my mechanic, and she also sometimes mentioned her brother, Kyle. He hated school, hardly ever went and would instead spend his days at his dad's garage. So, instead of going to school, Kyle would ride his motorbike around Tameside. He started doing well in speedway but had a shoulder injury, so his dad brought him in so I could help with his rehabilitation.

During that, I showed him speed and reaction work, which was just what he needed for the moment the gates lift at the start of a race. You've got to be so quick in your reactions to get to the front right away and that's what we worked on. Kyle got on the England team and did brilliantly, becoming British Under-21 champion. He later introduced me to a guy called Charlie Wright, who began working with me and has since been British champion and went to the world championships, so I've had a lot more acclaim for my work with him.

Working with both of them, and all the other athletes, has been an absolute privilege. I think back to the melting pot of talent in the lab. There was a time when I had a speedway champion working with the taekwondo world number one, surrounded by professional footballers, and they all wanted to do speed and reaction work for so many different ultimate uses. It was marvellous, seeing these different brains processing exercises in different ways for different ends: either hurtling round a dirt track at 70 miles per hour without brakes, or trying to kick somebody's head off, or sprinting towards a ball and half-volleying it into a very specific target.

Whatever their discipline, whether it was the Warrington Wolves squad or Mike Eade, a boxing and kickboxing champion, you see all their differences but you can actually train them in a fairly similar manner. The trick is to make sure that their mind is on their sport. Their brain has to relate the action to the sport in which it's going to be used. The sessions were incredible with those groups together. Aaron was accustomed to kicking heads, not balls, but even to this day when he joins in shooting practice or head tennis with the footballers, he's right up there with them. He often beats the professionals – not that any of them ever dare object!

I never go looking for opportunities, they always just knock on my door. There have been times when very famous people have been on the other side of that door. Sir Clive Woodward, England's World Cup-winning rugby union coach, came and spent time at the lab and we discussed various methodologies. At one stage, Powerade got in touch and asked if Michael and I could lead a training session for journalists out in Barcelona, with the added bonus that Andres Iniesta would also be partaking. The drills, planned out by our Michael, culminated in Iniesta teeing up each and every journalist to recreate his goal against Holland which won Spain the 2010 World Cup.

* * *

With all this going on, I didn't have the time to miss United. I was too excited and engaged in what I was learning and teaching to be concerned with looking back at the past.

That said, a familiar face from United did come back on the scene in 2013 and provide me with one of the greatest highlights of my coaching career.

Darren Fletcher, one of my best friends at the club, had been through a terrible time with ulcerative colitis, a debilitating bowel disease which had wreaked havoc on his career. Since I'd left Carrington, he'd been through two enforced career breaks in the space of two seasons and undergone surgery to correct the problem. He had been told by more than one medical professional that his career was essentially over.

After his surgery, Fletch had occasionally popped into Carrington and found everyone to be predictably nice towards him. Thing is, he didn't want pity. I think he worried about it. He'd never pitied himself during the whole ordeal because he's such a strong character. He got in touch and asked if he could come to the lab and train with me for a while before going back into regular training at Carrington. He wanted to be in better shape so that he wasn't starting from the bottom rung of the ladder.

I spoke with United's doctor, Steve McNally, to square it all off with him, and Darren came down. I had to be very careful, of course. Sprints, jumps and other explosive moves could have been damaging to somebody with such a sensitive bowel condition, so I had to bleed him in, doing things that the body could easily overcome and then the next day he could go again. It basically entailed using the overload training principle – steadily increasing the burden on your athlete – albeit in micro amounts.

In my own mind, I knew it was a long shot for Darren to get back to playing regularly for United, but I had previous experience of his determination. His mentality was strong as hell. From being this skinny young lad who went through lots of little injury setbacks along the way, he'd proven to himself time and time again that he could overcome the odds. He made it clear in his first session that he was determined to do so again and there was no reason to doubt what he was saying.

If it wasn't going to happen, I'd have told him that it was a lost cause, but there was no need to because with somebody like Fletch, you just let them go, they'll prove it to themselves and prove it to you. He came down for around six weeks and it was just brilliant to have a person like that in the gym on a regular basis; a top-level athlete who was fighting to get back to the top. It didn't matter who else was in the gym with him, however many other athletes were there, he was a pleasure around the place.

Great attitude, as ever. Hard work, as ever. Bit by bit, he did it and it was just amazing to see. Speaking as a rehab coach, you never reach a point where you think: *he's going to make it, it's going to happen.* You only think in steps. *Step one, this is what we do; step two, this is what we do; step three: now we go in this direction because we've been through steps one and two.* The end game isn't in your mind, it's the next step. That's the job.

In 2013, Darren made it back to United's first team. He was fit enough to play all the time so, when Louis van Gaal came in as manager and didn't plan to use him too often, Darren left to join West Brom in 2015 and, between his time there and a subsequent spell at Stoke, he made 112 successive Premier League appearances – becoming only the eighth player in history to pass 100. He proved everybody wrong.

I've seen a lot of people go through a lot of adversity. I would say what Darren did was easily the biggest step I've seen someone take, in terms of being really, really poorly and making it back to the very top of sport. For Darren to go from such a high to such a low and claw his way back up, I just think it was unfathomably courageous. For me, it was great to think of him as the kid I'd trained at 16 and then see what an incredible adult he had grown into. For him to come to me in the first place was an absolute honour. I've always said that the most honourable thing I've had in my career is people entrusting their kids' development to me, but for Darren to have all those staff available to him at United and to come to me instead, that is a similar privilege. It just meant so much.

While there were permanent reminders of my time at United, either through old acquaintances getting in touch or simply through a glance at the pictures on my lab walls, the only time I missed being at the club was when Ole Gunnar

Solskjaer was confirmed as the club's permanent manager in early 2019. He came to see me that spring, ostensibly for a brew and a catch-up, but soon he asked me about going back to the club and, as much as I wanted to, I just couldn't bring myself to leave my place.

I didn't feel I could let down my existing clients, including a couple of lads who I'd started training relatively recently: Mark Hagan and Thomas Traynor. I was also training their wives and children – six kids in total – and the pair of them had become investors in the lab. Having regularly complained about the state of the facility, which was in need of a serious facelift when they first arrived, Mark and Thomas paid to have it spruced up and built a structure for major developments. Some very exciting opportunities were already in the pipeline, including a gym franchise which is now underway in Egypt, and I just couldn't walk away.

So, just like when Brian Kidd first called all those years ago, I turned United down. This time I told Ole that our Michael would be a perfect fit instead. He was more than capable, he was available for the first time in a long time, so within a few weeks, Michael was back at the club where his career began. Even though I knew the job was in safe hands, and even though I knew I couldn't bring myself to let down my investors and clients, I have to be honest and admit that I did pine to go back during that period, especially when Ole invited me into Carrington and I met everybody who worked there, including some who I'd worked with before, like Michael Carrick.

I'd trained Paul Pogba as a kid and he remembered me. He was big and strong when I trained him as a teenager, but he's even bigger and stronger now, let me tell you. I goaded him a little bit, betting him that he was soft these days, so he naturally took the bait and we ended up doing a little bit of boxing there and then. No pads or anything. Each of his hands were as big as my head, and he rained punches down on my hands with great power and ferocity.

I'm sure it meant very little to him, but it was a real throwback for me because loads of players in the gym gathered round to watch us, just like my first weeks at the club back in 2000 when I was sparring with Roy and Wes. Having received Ole's offer and been back to Carrington in the space of a few weeks, it was inevitable that I would have mixed emotions during that period. It was almost delayed grief, because I didn't miss it for the first eight years after I'd left the club, then everything came rushing back at once.

It's hard to fully describe that feeling, and the same applied when Cristiano Ronaldo re-joined United in the summer of 2021. I never really imagined that he would come back but, a couple of days after he arrived, Michael got in touch to say that Cristiano had been looking for me at Carrington.

What a moment in time that was for me. I dare say it was strange for Cristiano to wander back into the gym and find himself working with my son. I'd be lying if I said I hadn't let my mind wander and imagine what it would have been like to train Cristiano again, had I accepted Ole's offer to return, but I'm more than happy with how things have panned out since I left United.

When I juxtaposed my career at the club and my career post-departure, the two periods were different in obvious ways but similar in probably the most important. Both gave me unforgettable times and priceless lessons which have shaped the person and coach that I am today.

CHAPTER 29

Animal Magic

*"I genuinely think this is the best
training method to take us towards
unlocking superpowers in regular humans."*

When people come into my lab, they're greeted by a host of familiar faces. I spent years working with Lewis Travis, a midfielder at Blackburn, and his father, Darren, was very grateful for the impact it was having on Lewis's career, to the point that he kept having images blown up and printed onto glass. While I was training Lewis, his dad would be busy adorning the walls, completely free of charge.

So, when you walk in, you'll see all the obvious faces: Keane, Ronaldo, Scholes, Giggs, van Nistelrooy and so on. I often see people walking along the wall and taking in all the pictures to see who they recognise. They often stop when they get to a certain point.

"Mick, why are these here?"

Among all those familiar figures, I have two photos of animals: one of a peregrine falcon and one of a cheetah. In my post-United years, and with a lot of help from more technically-minded folk, I started a website to act as a compendium for my coaching theories. I named it *Seed of*

Speed, because of the recognition that we need to train the brain, rather than the body, because the brain controls the body. So, the brain is the origin – or seed – of speed.

In the case of those two animals I have on my wall, the most important parts of both animals are the eyes. Their vision creates the rest of it. The vision makes the cheetah the fastest land animal and the falcon the fastest animal in the world. These animals are an evolutionary triumph. The falcon can see its prey from a mile away and can swoop down towards it at speeds reaching 220mph.

Think about how big the prey is going to appear from a mile away. The cheetah sees a gazelle and, from half a mile away, spots a weakness. The cheetah can run at 70 miles per hour, but gazelles are fast too, and the chase is hardly taking place on a bowling green. It's an undulating path lined with obstacles and potholes, and that pathway is guided by vision. As the cheetah gets closer, it has picked its spot, goes to top speed and usually catches its prey. These traits have come about through vision and these machines have evolved over millions of years.

The brain – whether in an animal or a human – was designed with movement in mind. If you take movement without vision, then these animals can't do what they do. I apply the same principles when I train athletes in my lab. I still use the Neurotracker with every client, plus the D2, a machine whereby the athlete has to tap various buttons as they light up in a totally random order. Development of the visual field is the pathway to overall development. I prioritise making their vision as efficient as it can possibly be, so that it can unlock their brain's potential.

The next step in the process is to unlock emotion. You

don't see top-level athletes performing at their best without emotion. If you freeze the action as a boxer knocks out their opponent, the emotion which has powered that punch will be written over their face. That knockout blow has come from a place of emotional, spiritual power, not just raw physicality brought about by bicep curls or chest presses.

The more emotion you can stir in your athlete, the better you can coach them. The better the vision of your athlete, the better they can become. That's why my method – the splice training I mentioned when discussing Ruud van Nistelrooy's impact on my career – is about stimulating the athlete's brain, vision and emotion at the same time.

I think that this differentiates my approach to coaching because I've never heard another coach talk about this kind of methodology. I've spent decades trying to understand the brain and its importance in controlling all the mechanisms, but also recognising the subsequent importance of vision and emotion to harnessing the power of the brain.

I didn't start out with a plan to develop my own method of coaching so I could give it a name. I just spent a long time working with a lot of people, learning a lot of lessons and spending a long time breaking down and understanding the things I was seeing.

Take our Michael, my original crash test dummy, as an example. One of the most important things I learnt very early in my career was Olympic lifting, because you're using strength, of course, but you're using speed and you're also jumping. When I introduced that to Michael, even though he was only small in stature as a kid, he began entering weightlifting competitions, he trained in boxing, and I could see the power and determination and real desire that the training had provoked within him. On top of that, he was a better-rounded, more able athlete who could lift heavy weights, jump higher and lift faster, and everything came together bit by bit. While I would do some things differently with him if I could do it all again, it was certainly a success because he ended up playing for Manchester United despite not being an unbelievably gifted footballer.

It's an unbelievable story, like someone wrote a script for him, but it comes from righting wrongs. When you take an athlete with inabilities, work on those deficiencies and fix them, it allows them to show a lot more ability. Mike Eade, for example, went for the world kickboxing championship five times without winning it, came to work with me and won silver after a couple of months, but then the next year, after fully realising his inefficiencies and spending time putting them right, went on to win the world championship in Montreal.

As a coach, I learnt from what was working and what wasn't working, and it was very apparent very quickly that pulling in one exercise with another and knitting them together was a very successful approach. This is quantum consciousness, the ability to fix things together so they work in harmony and extract the maximum power from the brain. If you think in terms of boxing, you may be throwing punches and suddenly take evasive action because your opponent is throwing punches at you. In that split second you decide to change. To be able to make those decisions so quickly, you need to do it without requiring the time to think through your options.

Over time, as a coach, you realise what you've been seeing in your athletes: the blending of these vibratory signals going through their brains, through this consciousness, and because everything's being done together, they can slip from strength to speed to agility to power to skill to vision and decision-making. That's what my method is all about. This is what I do now in my lab with all my athletes in all kinds of sports. I've been doing it for years to great effect and I genuinely think that this is the best training method to take us towards unlocking superpowers in regular humans.

CHAPTER 30

Higher Power

"Living in the Trafford and Tameside area meant I was never short of the chance to go and have a long stroll in the rain."

In 2017, I went to see the doctor.

My wife, Tina, had spotted a mole on my back which she felt looked sinister and, moreover, had changed in appearance over the previous weeks. I also felt run down and had a heavy cold, so I acquiesced and visited a professional.

He had news for me.

I was diagnosed with a very aggressive melanoma skin cancer, which I was told could quickly invade my heart, lungs and liver, so I needed to start chemotherapy immediately at The Christie, one of Europe's leading cancer hospitals.

This news was delivered very monochromatically, with a splash of colour provided when the doctor added that I would need to have a large amount of skin removed from my back, which would be replaced via plastic surgery using skin from my backside. For good measure, I'd have lymph nodes removed so that the medical professionals could assess how deep the infection had gone.

Many times down the years, I've had gym clients mention in passing that they're about to go for a check-up, only to subsequently inform me that they have been diagnosed with cancer and given months to live. They've been through chemotherapy, surgery, and they've steadily wasted away before dying.

So, learning that I had cancer in my body brought me to a fork in the road. I could either hand over control and agree to let medical professionals do whatever they saw fit to do, or I could damn well fix my sights and decide what I needed to do to get myself healthy again.

I felt like it was God tapping me on the shoulder and saying: "What about you? Always telling people what to do to sort themselves out. Have you sorted yourself out? Here you go: cancer. Go and sort that out, you bad-tempered old git."

So, let me give you the backstory of God and I.

When I was in my 20s, I read a lot of self-help books. I was absolutely fixated on becoming the best version of myself that I could be. I remember reading *Psycho-Cybernetics* by Maxwell Maltz, *Think and Grow Rich* by Napoleon Hill, *Pyramid Power* by Greg Nielsen and Max Toth, then later the likes of *Men are from Mars, Women are from Venus* by John Gray.

What I remember taking away most from all of those is that each of them points straight at you as the only source of your success. Some of those books are old now, but that core point remains absolutely true: life hands you nothing that you don't make happen.

As part of my ongoing self-development, I learned meditation, starting with the candle flame method. It's as simple as it sounds: stare at the flame and give your sight and attention over to nothing but that flame. That taught me how to focus on whatever was in my sight. I learned breathing meditation which taught me to control my breath, especially in tense situations. I listened to vocal and musical meditations that helped me to focus on what people were saying or trying to say and my interpretations of their vocal emotions.

The books taught me how to think about what I deeply desired and form a plan of how to achieve it. I was incessant in my reading but, whenever I looked through the shelves in libraries or book shops, I avoided books about religion at all costs. I worried that my subconscious could be overwhelmed by thoughts and ideas that could be dangerous to my development.

In my younger days I had been to church and I'd read some of the Bible, but I also linked that to some horrific nightmares that I used to have. I'd literally be chased by devils and demons which, I can tell you, is as utterly terrifying as it sounds. When I awoke, the worry I associated with religion would plague me. Also, certain aspects didn't stack up for me. It always stood out to me that 'thou shalt not bow down to idols', yet it seemed to be exactly what people were doing. The Bible said to keep the sabbath day – Saturday – free for prayer, but Sunday school and church services were on a Sunday. I was told that the church is where God is, but I could never see him when I walked through the doors. People said I had to trust in God but I didn't sense God anywhere around. I wasn't having any book trying to convince me with something I couldn't see, let alone sense.

As I aged, having children heightened my sense of responsibility and my desire to keep improving for the good of everyone around me. The better, more knowledgeable person I was, I reasoned, the better parent I'd be. The more knowledge I amassed and the more I harnessed the power of meditation, the deeper my thinking became and I became increasingly impressed by the minds of the people who were writing what I was reading.

After a few years of endless reading, I realised that fewer and fewer books were appealing to me. The books I hadn't read all seemed to centre on God, Christ or religion and I just did not want to go there. One day, I was reading a book – I forget exactly which one – when the author recommended reading Matthew, Mark, Luke and John, each in one sitting, and promised that it would change your life forever. Against all my best judgement, I took the plunge and began reading the entire Bible. I read all four gospels, then all the 750,000 words that the Bible contained and, once I was in, there was no looking back.

At this point I should stress that I am not attempting to convert anybody. Each person has their own faith and I respect that. I'm simply retracing my steps and sharing my journey. If religion absolutely does nothing for you, by all means skip ahead.

For me, one life ended and suddenly I was in a new life. I was around 30 when I started reading the Bible. Everything I had taken from the other books involved the five senses of sight, sound, touch, smell and taste and the manipulation of all those with a brain that is capable of so much more. The Bible spoke about spirituality, which was the main difference between the books written by man and the book written by God. The spirit cannot be discerned by our five senses. So, what is spirit? How can we know what is spiritual? What will spiritual knowledge give us in terms of making our lives better and more fulfilling? These were the questions I was left asking.

Whilst reading the Bible, the first thing that struck me was that God appeared to want structure and discipline with a mind that acknowledges man's ability to fail but allows the opportunity to try again when the fault was recognised. That was something that I recognised was of absolute necessity when coaching children. Failure led to emotional outbursts, which had to be controlled for any progress to be made. When I was coaching a group or class of children, if there was no structure or rules, there would be no learning. There had to be discipline of my mind to keep to the plan and discipline of the kids' minds to work together or all our efforts would end fruitlessly.

Recognising hierarchy became a valuable aid to asking children how to behave. If you have 15 kids in a group, three at one end will mess about and be a waste of time, three out the other end will be hard working and diligent. I'd ask the other nine: "Who do you think will make the most progress? Go and find where you want to be and your commitment to your decision will tell you where you are headed." I think parents brought their kids to me more for my discipline than my coaching of exercise. Most of the kids who came to train with me of their own volition did so because they knew I wouldn't let them get away with their own frailty; I would make them mentally stronger.

As I led students to become more aware of their senses to improve their performance, I wondered about the role of the spirit. Over the course of five years, I read the Bible three times, cover to cover. There's a fair bit to take in, after all, so putting together the information I was receiving took time, especially while combining it with the instruction of mental and physical development and layering down the aspects I was learning. I was combining it all with experience to really understand that if students were to gain from my sessions, they had to recognise my ideas and techniques.

As they developed, I was asking them to explain the experience they had gained. I'm always asking my students to talk to me about what we were doing and what we were developing. This was done using my most important tool for student development: the consultation. I realised that the consultation is of absolute necessity to truly understand what is required by any student to truly make the work they do with you productive.

The Bible talks of King Solomon, son of King David (of David and Goliath fame), asking God for wisdom above all things because he was going to be the king of Israel and wisdom was what he needed most to be able to rule successfully. The Bible says that God was so pleased with Solomon asking for wisdom instead of riches, power or long life, that He blessed Solomon with such wisdom that made him the wisest man that has ever lived. How I longed, over so many years, for just a little wisdom to help my beloved children. Even today, when I pray to God in my private place, wisdom is always at the front of my mind.

* * *

Once I recognised that the consultation was my best tool in coaching, but the wisdom to use the knowledge gained from the consultation was more important than the consultation itself, I could see that I was looking at spiritual things on a much higher level. I needed this wisdom, so I read an extreme amount of spiritual literature over many years.

When I was 37, I went to Israel with my daughter Mandy to go and see the Bible lands, where Jesus was said to have been born and killed. I was interested, but sceptical. Given the volume of sightseers and holidaymakers being told the stories, I thought that perhaps it was just people selling a story to boost tourism. Nevertheless, I still had this passion for what Jesus was supposed to have stood for and what he meant. The words attributed to him that I listened to made sense to me.

While we were there, I spoke with a guide who recommended that I be baptised. I had been christened as a kid, but having a cross marked out in water on my forehead before I could process sights or sounds hardly felt like a lifelong commitment to the cause.

"I haven't got a religion," I explained. "I just believe in Jesus Christ and the words attributed to him."

He asked me a few questions about the Bible, I answered them and he said: "You probably know more than most of these people here. Would you like to be baptised to no particular religion?"

I agreed, as long as it wasn't to a specific church, and ended up in a crowd of about 20 people on a beautiful day on the banks of the River Jordan. Everyone else wore white, I was in a yellow t-shirt and I was baptised as a Christian of no particular faith.

Among people who have been baptised, I've heard of some saying they saw Jesus afterwards, or God came into their life at that moment. Nothing came into my life at that moment apart from huge fish biting my legs. *Get off, you bastard, I'm being baptised*, I remember thinking. Hardly an epiphany.

I had envisaged gaining confidence and wisdom before I'd even dried off, but it didn't happen that way. A cleansing isn't instant, instead it filters through, and over a period of time I think it was one of those things that led to me becoming deeply into meditation. It was almost like it filtered into me that something had happened and it's always about getting into people's minds to make them think differently.

I'm part of a church now, but even in the years when I wouldn't term myself religious, I still learnt a lot from the Bible. Even when I was hugely sceptical of whether or not there was a Jesus Christ, I still read some books of the Bible 30 times, because whether you believe in God, Jesus, the spirit realm, the afterlife or anything at all, there is a blueprint for life in there which leads you down a good path. As such, I had always prayed. I'd always recognised, through periods with and without religion in my life, that there is both good and evil in the world, and I preferred to be on the good side.

So, when diagnosed with cancer, I prayed.

As I prayed, I felt feelings that invoked some of my deepest memories and scars. Suddenly I remembered rolling down the steep hills outside my first house; I remembered my first romantic thoughts about the lady across the road while she helped me draw battleships; I remembered being told off because I'd been caught eating bread that I was supposed to be feeding to chickens in a nearby coop; I remembered my mother giving birth to a stillborn baby in our front room; I remembered vivid nightmares and daymares as a child of being thrown onto an open fire; I remembered being so frightened by *The Exorcist* that I bought a Bible and cross to keep with me; I remembered living in a Salford boarding house during my apprenticeship where I was looked after by a petrifying hunchback.

These experiences – which sound strange but are all

absolutely true – showed me how powerful emotion can be in my makeup, and why I need to hear people's stories during their consultation, so that I can discover their emotion.

I remembered so many feelings after that diagnosis, but the overriding one which kept coming back, which consumed me, was one of pure, cold terror. The fear you have as a child.

The day I was diagnosed with cancer was exactly six months after Tina and I had married. We'd been together since August 2006 and living together for years. Re-marrying was never really on my radar but, having fallen deeper into religion during the course of the relationship, I realised that we were living in sin and I asked her to marry me (I can't think why she didn't see me as a romantic, on reflection). She was my best friend and we worked really hard together. Her acupuncture and massage business operated out of my gym, Rocky loved us both, so we were spending a lot of time around each other. Being entirely useless unless the whole guestlist required a workout plan, I stood by while Tina organised the entire wedding. She did a sensational job and we had a perfect wedding day.

Not long afterwards, I met a man called Robert, a minister for a church group I had been part of for at least a year. After decades of searching, I had found a church which remained true to the Bible and respected the sabbath. When I study something, it's my way to go in deep, so I fully immersed myself in the group. Robert had recently suffered a stroke and was very poorly, so I offered him some help with his rehabilitation.

By the end of our work together, Robert had made enormous progress and had the full use of his body once again. During one of his regular visits to Manchester, after

I'd been diagnosed, I told him about my situation. As a fully baptised minister in the church, he offered to anoint me. He also gave me lots of spiritual advice and some deep scientific studies on cancer that he had found after a lot of digging. Alongside counselling, anointment and prayer, I also threw myself into the deep study of health.

I found my thoughts going back to conversations I'd had down the years with Trevor Lea, United's nutritionist. I also revisited the fundamentals that, as staff, we'd taken for granted when preparing every single footballer. Uppermost importance was given to football skill, then athleticism. Then, beyond that, we would look at proper diet, proper sleep, living the right lifestyle and thinking the right thoughts so that they're in line with making yourself better than you were before.

I took all these principles in mind for myself. I was closing in on 60 years of age. I had a choice between handing myself over to a standard set of procedures which would be out of my hands, or looking at myself and actually doing what I'd been telling other people to do for years.

I had to strip it all down. At the core of it all, there was something inside me that wasn't working right. I had to get to the bottom of that. What isn't working right and how do I fix it? First and foremost, my pH level was too acidic. Why? I looked at the way I was running my life. The main thing that causes acidity inside the body is stress, so I had to take down my stress levels. The other aspect that heightened my acidity levels was that I was always working late at the gym, so I'd then have a late tea and a glass of wine, then I'd be in bed within maybe 20 minutes. Too often I'd literally crawl to bed, absolutely exhausted, with chicken and red wine in my belly.

My acid levels were dangerously high, so that needed fixing. I looked into that and realised that my adrenal cortex – part of the adrenal gland, just above my kidneys – was under such pressure that it was badly stressed. I researched how to sort that out, what lifestyle changes I needed to make and what nutrients it needed to sort itself out. That meant going almost entirely vegan in a short space of time. The local greengrocer's shelves were emptied. One of my clients, Mark Hagan, would literally bring a crate of vegetables and fruit along every time he came to train or to drop his kids off. I had a kitchen put in the back of the gym so that I could cook food from scratch.

Then I looked at inflammation. That's so important to understand in overcoming stress in the body and the mind. Inflammation stops your nerves working properly. For years, I'd struggled with my grip, and I'd always put that down to decades of wear and tear lifting weights or holding boxing pads while people smacked me about. It turned out that wasn't the case. It was just inflammation affecting the nerves. So, I needed a plan to remove the inflammation. Again, I had to ask: why has it happened and how can I overcome it? It requires a change in the nervous system, especially in the emotional system, a change in the diet and then a change in the type of work I was doing.

Every instinct I had just told me to take control, start living my life the right way and sort out all the shit and poison that I'd been putting into my body. Rather than feed the cancer, I took away all the foods and drinks that were causing my system problems. I spoke with some of my most intelligent associates, including Lee Sidebottom, a research engineer and former colleague of mine, and Jocelyn Faubert, the renowned neuroscientist at Montreal University, and took their advice on board. I look back now and think: *You fool. You took your finger off the button.* Not because I didn't care about myself, but just because I was fixated on working every available hour and that cost me the balance in my life. It was just like when my appendix burst: I'd overloaded myself and paid the price.

Within three months of my diagnosis, I had changed every single type of food and drink that entered my system.

With my faith and all the knowledge I was amassing about my health, I felt empowered and ready for what lay ahead. You always hear about the fight against cancer, but spiritually I felt encouraged not to fight, to instead turn away from that conflict. Like Daniel in the lions' den, turn away from what is frightening you and don't fear anything, God will handle it.

So I started making changes. Rocky never had so many walks as he did during the next few weeks. I'd take him to heavily wooded areas like Sale Water Park, often when it was hammering it down with rain. Again, this was based on research. Walking while surrounded by trees heightened the amount of oxygen I'd be taking in, and that increased even further when it was raining.

Living in the Trafford and Tameside area meant that I was never short of the chance to go and have a long stroll in the rain. I found it so peaceful. There was no stress or worry at all during those walks, just me and my mate enjoying our time.

Things started happening. Quickly. In the space of six to eight weeks, I lost a shedload of weight through the changes to my diet, I felt a lot better. I ignored virtually everything I was told during my diagnosis, ignored repeated requests for appointments and, I daresay, generally pissed off the medical staff with my behaviour. I was determined to go my own way with my God and make my own informed decisions about what was right for my body.

In 2021, I went to see the doctor again.

I had no sign of cancer in my body and was signed off from the hospital.

CHAPTER 31

The Next Generation

"Any child gives their parents highs and lows. When I look back over my life, I think my greatest moments have come from my kids' successes."

There's a well-established trope of 'the absent father' whenever a marriage ends in divorce and children remain living with their mother.

Perhaps it's partially guilt at being the one who left the family home and moved elsewhere. Even if you move around the corner and go back every day to see the kids, even if you still see them every day to take them to school or train them, or even if you end up working in the same football club as them, there are still certain givens that come with the territory: assumption by others that you're a deadbeat dad, and paranoia on your part that everyone assumes you're a deadbeat dad.

I left because I was constantly being told by Sue that I wasn't good enough to be in that house. Three times I was kicked out and asked back, and for my own sanity and self-respect I couldn't go back a fourth time, so that was it. Yes, I left, but

I know in my heart that my divorce had no impact on my parenting, even though it hurt me a lot more than I allowed myself to feel. I honestly don't know if the kids ever heard the full story of the split before I wrote this book. Perhaps now they'll see another dimension to the story.

As you get older, you can't help but look back on how things have panned out and I know how it might look from the outside: shouty man shouts at his children so they all follow in his footsteps out of obedience and terror. I can honestly say that, as far as I'm concerned, there was no pressure from me on them to do well at sports or become coaches.

I'm very mindful, by the way, that I've not properly introduced everybody. As a family with a good amount of sporting success, we've had some media attention at times with interviews for *Muscle & Fitness* magazine, among others. Mandy never gets a light shone on her.

I had a horribly flippant attitude towards this in Mandy's early years. She's a girl, I'm a bloke so, when she was young, I basically left Sue to look after her because I had no clue about females. I was comfortable and capable looking after the lads, but I thought it would be better for her development to spend time with her mum playing with dolls. How wrong I was. Mandy showed her character by deciding that she didn't want to play with dolls. Instead, she wanted to play with weights and sporting equipment in the gym. That's what impressed me most about her when she was younger. She chose to come down to the gym with me and the boys instead of staying at home with her mum.

When I was bringing lads down from Moss Side on a Friday night, she'd be there. Her strength of character was there from an early age, along with a clear determination to get stuck in. She made her presence known, everyone knew and respected her and that's the case to this day. When I go around Olympic these days, after all these years, there's a lot of respect for Mandy. She's an excellent coach – she's trained Britain's Strongest Woman, among others – but what stands out to me is that Olympic is in incredibly safe hands with her. She knows the business very well. Around the gym, people often go up to her and ask her advice, which is a throwback to my early days at Shapes, but the making of Mandy is not me. She fed off some of the things I said and did, but is very much of her own making. She was a sensational swimmer in her younger years, but she put her athletic ambitions on the back-burner when she had her daughter Katie at just 16.

Now, Katie has turned out to be an incredible athlete and a lot of that is down to Mandy pushing her. Katie – a lot like Mark used to be – was a non-athlete until she decided to be a boxer. She just totally changed her mindset. Just like I was always at the gym and Mandy wanted to be there when she was a kid, Katie always wanted to be around Mandy at the gym. She trained like Mandy, made friends her own age at the gym and things just took off. She latched onto boxing, loved it and now she's very, very good.

Getting in that ring and slugging it out isn't for the faint-hearted. Training is all well and good because punchbags and focus mitts don't hit back, but getting in the ring and taking a smack to the face is an acid test for any young boxer. Katie has had quite a few fights already and has won a few medals. She's technically very good from what I've seen of her in training, but I can't comment on any of her fights because I've not been able to bring myself to go. As much as I love her – as I love all of my grandkids – I have to support her in spirit because I don't like the idea of seeing her being punched in the face. I love the fact that boxing has got her in great shape and given her such purpose, but I don't see myself being ringside anytime soon.

It might look like Katie is carrying on the family name in competitive sports these days, but I don't think there has ever been any pressure or weight that has accompanied being a Clegg. Michael wanted to be a footballer so I helped him to be a footballer. None of the others were pressured. Mark played basketball at school and naturally evolved – my only input to that was to put up a proper basketball post rather than sticking a net on a wall, which isn't relevant to how basketball is played. Having a post was massive for Mark's development. He then saw that weightlifting would help his basketball and he ended up falling into that.

There was no sense that he had to succeed in sport or he wouldn't be as good as Michael. Steven came along, did everything that Michael and Mark were doing and had no real firm direction in his ambitions until United handed him a five-year contract. Opportunities arose and they took them.

The same goes for Shaun, who is also overdue a proper introduction. Mark opened up a junior weightlifting club, Shaun enrolled in that and was fantastic. Mark was always Shaun's hero, not me, Michael or Steven. As he grew up, Shaun went on to basically become the wild child of British weightlifting. He smoked, he drank, he wasn't technically the very best in the squad, but he had this mental ability to overcome problems. He knew his shortcomings but knew that he could compensate by putting in more effort than anybody else could. He had the heartbreak of being selected for Team GB at the 2012 London Olympics, then deselected, before he went on to compete at the Commonwealth Games in 2014. Overall, he won 14 national titles and set 16 individual records at various age and weight groups – no doubt his favourite being when he overtook a record of Mark's which had stood for 15 years!

Shaun retired from competitive weightlifting at 21 and, while it took him a while to adapt to life after the sport, he has since found a bit more peace in himself. He's now back training with me at the lab and I just leave him to it. I'll help and advise whenever I'm required, but I'm not going to put pressure on him to be any specific kind of coach.

* * *

My relationships with my kids are complicated, which is as much my fault as theirs. I don't like pushing myself on people, so I'll quite often leave them to their own devices. The capacity in which I come into contact with them is almost entirely gym-based. As well as seeing Shaun at the lab, I see the others all the time, often in Olympic, which is now co-managed by Mandy, Steven and Mark. Michael's busy with United but comes to see me when he can. Since we're all coaches, even though we've worked together for decades, we often disagree.

For example, Michael wandered into the lab during an early training session with Thomas, one of the investors in my gym, who had a very bad back. When Michael saw the state of Thomas, he posited that I was mad for working with him because I could do some serious damage. I had total faith that I could overcome those issues and, within long, we'd fixed the problems. There are undoubtedly loads of examples of me being wrong and the kids being right, but the point is that we don't always agree and nor do we need to.

Over time, I've increasingly tended to listen to their problems more than doling out advice and solutions. That's one area where I would say that I could have done better as a parent. I think I gave good structure and I really worked hard to give the kids all that was necessary, all the materials, all the time, but I was probably too hard on their minds when they were younger.

My own childhood wasn't horrific, but it wasn't great. My mum and dad used to argue all the time. They were alcoholics and we'd move from place to place. I found them very difficult to be with. I never really had a good relationship with my dad and at times I hated my mother, despite the fact that I was told I was her favourite child.

That wasn't nice for my brother and sister, thinking I was the favourite, so it was a bad position to be put into. I never understood my parents. They did and said too many things that weren't good for our morale as children and didn't give us the chance to feel good about ourselves. I think they made bad decisions due to alcohol. I was 29 when dad died of alcohol poisoning, 42 when mum did the same. They both died at 65. My mum remarried and you'd have hoped she would have learnt lessons from my dad's death, but she didn't.

My mind, because of all that, became hardened, so when I put something in place for my kids, I expected them to respect it and work hard with it, and if they didn't then I was onto them. I wasn't just taking them to play sports, I would ferry them everywhere they went and even take their girlfriends home. I was up at all hours, never having any time for myself, always running around after them, and having that attitude towards them made me think that they really needed to put their heart and soul into what they were doing. I felt like I deserved them to do well in what they were doing because I'd worked so hard to enable it. I saw it as payback. I was probably too hard on them and I don't think they liked me for it.

If they had a problem and went to Sue, they'd talk about it and that would be the end of it. If they came to me with a problem, I'd plan out the solution with them, which wasn't always the right route to take. They probably needed more empathy from me. I can't be telling people how to run their lives, but back then I thought I should be because I had responsibility for them. Now, when somebody – be it one of the kids, a client or a friend – comes to me and asks me what they should do about something, then I have to get a lot more information from them so that I fully understand what they're asking for. I'm a lot softer, a lot less prescriptive than I was.

How do you assess what influence you've had on your kids' lives? To me it's simple: if you can see what you do in what they do, then you've got something to compare. They've been athletes at the best level. Manchester United. World championships. European championships. That part is incomparable because they've done things that I could never have done and they've got huge experiences as athletes, but now they're all coaches as well.

When it comes to that aspect, what's absolutely key to me

is that they're not stagnant in their minds and thinking: *I'll just follow my dad.* I would never want that. You give your kids information, you show them a leading light to get them somewhere, but you don't want to be their life. You want them to have a life and create themselves. You're not there to tell them to do what you've done; they've got to do what their hearts and minds feel like doing.

They're all at various stages of carving out their own pathways, all split between their late 20s and early 40s. Nobody knows what the future holds but, when I look at their journeys so far, it's important for me to spell out how proud I am of them and how grateful I am for what they've done for me. I've guided them as best I can, but they've been incredible guides for me too. I couldn't have asked for more than I've gotten from my kids. They have been the ultimate weapon, if you like, to work with. They would listen, they would try new things and go along with new methods that I imagined. They gave me everything that they could, so I know that I'm very, very fortunate in that because they backed me up on everything.

Any child gives their parents highs and lows. When I look back over my life so far, I think my greatest moments have come from my kids' successes. If you're in a situation where you can feel pressure bearing down on you and you get a good outcome, that feels incredible, and I've had so many instances of that feeling with my kids. I think back to all the times I've had my heart in my mouth while Mark has been in a weightlifting competition or Michael was lining up at Old Trafford, for instance, but that feeling when they perform well and win, those moments have been probably the purest joy I've experienced.

So, however much people might think my kids owe me for their careers in sport and coaching, I owe them just as much and more besides.

CHAPTER 32

Listen

"I've made more difference to careers over a cup of tea than I have by prescribing perfect-form squats, shoulder presses or lateral raises."

I was nine years old when The Beatles released *When I'm 64*. I just couldn't imagine being that old.

Now that I'm there, I think back to a line from the song.

"Send me a postcard, drop me a line; stating point of view; indicate precisely what you mean to say; yours sincerely, wasting away."

So, as I search for closing thoughts, I'm mindful of how lucky I've been, not least in recent years. I've survived a major health scare and, even though I'm now a little old fella, remain extremely busy with clients. The pandemic has prompted something of a rethink in my approach but, with the help of more technically-minded people, I've been introduced to coaching over Zoom and it has opened up some intriguing new opportunities.

There's no such thing as an average day. I've never had a conveyor belt of footballers coming in and out of my lab, there has always been variety in the people I've trained. Now, I don't even necessarily have just athletes. For instance, I'm able to hop online to train Sara, a Portuguese actress living in London, then I might have a couple of youth team footballers mid-morning, and after lunch I can coach Venezia's first team players over Zoom before welcoming Rosie, a wonderful little girl overcoming cerebral palsy. No two days are the same.

I've got a kid who comes to my lab every week. Daniel. He's 14. He lifts weights a lot heavier than 19-year-old lads who come at the same time. He smashes the football training against footballers.

The kid's a golfer.

That's how varied the world is.

So, do you think there's one method or ideology that suits every person, or even every athlete?

Before I started working with Venezia, I had a video call with club officials and I was told that they wanted visibility of all my routines for the next three months, so that they could work it in with the programmes they were putting together for the players.

Fair enough, I appreciated their need to plan. Problem was, I hadn't met any of the players yet, so I told them I didn't know what I'd be doing.

The officials were confused. "What does that matter? You know what to do with them."

"How could I possibly know what to do with them?"

"You're a coach, aren't you?"

"Yes, but that's not how I coach. That's why I'm different."

I'm sometimes asked if I'm a carrot coach or a stick coach. I hate that stupid question.

You have to be both, in different measures at different times. Sometimes you have to be heavy-handed with a mighty stick and offer a measly crumb of carrot, other times you hand them an enormous carrot and wield a tiny little stick. Each individual and each circumstance requires different combinations at different times.

It's like the nature/nurture debate. Are people more affected by factors which are inherited or acquired? Again, I see no point to it. Your genetic materials are there to be used, but only in whatever environment you occupy. Say person A has a genetic predisposition to easily gain muscle; if they're in a big, happy house with loads of high-quality food, what happens to them is going to turn out differently than if they were in a squalid, disruptive house with only a little poor-quality food.

You can look at a human being and categorise them by gender, age and so on, but when you come to standardise, it's pointless. Just as every snowflake and every grain of sand is different and has always been different since the beginning of time, so are people. Viewed from afar, you can recognise that they're all grains of sand or individual snowflakes. When you look closely, then you begin to see the differences.

You've got to take each person as an individual. I cannot stress that enough.

I've been doing that from the very start of my coaching career, and I think it stemmed from a very simple recognition: I don't have the answers, not yet. When you don't know them in advance, you have to work hard to find them out.

It wasn't something I purposely did when I went to United, it just seemed to come naturally. My first instinct when I met Roy Keane was to put his first rehab session on hold until I knew more about him, his injury, his background, his likes and his dislikes.

So, back in 2000, I wrote down a single sheet of notes about Roy, including a loose training plan. I wrote one for every single player because that initial consultation was absolutely paramount to the work we were going to do. Even then, however, that sheet was never used in terms of day-to-day activities. You might write down a training programme and then find out that Player A wasn't enjoying hip drives. Instead, they wanted their calves and ankles to be a lot stronger because they always felt like they were at risk of buckling as they were about to smash the ball. That stabilising and balancing foot is the one that's going to let them down, not the accuracy from the other foot. You're looking at all the things they need to work with from their emotional point of view.

You're finding out what drives them.

Then you amend your advice according to what they want and need, in the hope of sorting out their issue. If you do manage to sort it out with them, they don't think *what a great coach*, they think *it's good working with this guy*, because you can help them get to where they want to be. That's how you earn their trust.

Not everybody trains regularly over a span of years and years. You tend to find that a lot of people train for a while, then it fades away and they give up. That hasn't been the case so far in my career. A high volume of people in the area who I trained as kids still come to Olympic or the lab and, to me, that comes from doing it from a place of deep passion. They haven't learnt about training in a classroom, they've been asked to look within themselves and develop heartfelt knowledge and understanding of what they're doing and the reasons therein.

I don't know of anybody else who runs a gym in the same way that I do, because I cover so many different sports and I've been with so many different athletes who've done well, so I understand training from lots of different points of view. That doesn't mean for a second that I think I'm clever, because I'm not, but what it means is that every athlete who comes in, I'm able to hear their story and then, by finding out what they feel they need, then you give them what they need for them to be more effective in what they do. You can have your theories and preconceptions as to what you think they need, but if it isn't correlating with their mind and isn't in line with what they're thinking, then it'll never be as effective.

A consultation isn't necessarily sitting there with a pen and paper and taking notes about what you're being told. You can just sit there and be really interested in who they are, what they are, what they're trying to achieve and what their problem is. At United, people came to see me when things were going wrong, not always when everything was going right, and that's true until today. Back in 2000, I starting working with a playing squad that was doing really well. I'd like to think I did enhance what was going on at United but at the end of the day they were successful anyway. I didn't go in there, do my thing and then regard myself as a smart-arse. These were great players anyway. I didn't teach them anything, I was just learning from them by listening to their stories and wondering: *if there's a chance of helping them, how could I do it?*

That's why they're all over the walls of my gym, because they trained me. They trained me by showing me where they needed to go and what they needed to do to accomplish what they accomplished. They've led me down that track by talking to me, by having a consultation, by coming and seeing me after training. I've made more difference to careers over a cup of tea than I have by prescribing perfect-form squats, shoulder presses or lateral raises. You need a tiny insight, that's all. You say something, you get a little response, you start work and see how that response generates into something else. The hint that gets you started is the thin end of the wedge. You might detect that a kid who wants to be a footballer has better handling than footwork, and that sets them off down the career path of a rugby player.

Minute amounts of things that you can pick out can make a difference. Possibly down to the time I spent working with a hypnotist, I have this ability to see how you can turn somebody's mind from thinking one thing to thinking something else. With some people, you have to think of a story and hit them hard with it. Other times you have to tell them something bad about themselves. Or something glorious about themselves. Every person is so completely different and it's trying to get the right opinion, the right thoughts, the right methodology, just at the right time. That's very often how I feel when I'm meeting clients: that I'm looking for something that's important to them that I can trigger just enough to have a big effect.

The way to do that is so, so simple.

Shut up.

Listen.

Observe.

Understand.

See if there are any opportunities to be creative within that environment.

To me, it's all about listening to people so that you can decipher what they need. My entire career has been built on my ability to listen to somebody and pick things out that are important to them.

I want to see it from their point of view, not my point of view. It's ridiculous for me to think in terms of my point of view. Listen to theirs and then see where yours and theirs relate to each other. Then you've got a much mightier force to work with.

You don't even have to have a list of perfectly crafted questions to really understand people. Just shut your mouth and let them go. They'll ask the questions within that. Then, guess what you lead them to do: find the answers themselves. They ask you the questions, you lead them to the answers. Don't tell them; they have to find it themselves. It's not easy at all, because you've got to lead them into an area that you don't know.

You can't possibly know what's going on in their minds, but they will start to tell you while they're looking for answers, and all those answers are already there. All you can try to do is shine some light on them. When they answer it themselves, that's what makes them make progress. It's not you telling them what to do; it's their own realisation of what to do. Then they're going through the process themselves.

To me, that's not just the golden rule of coaching; it's a means of being the best human you can be and building the best relationships you can. If people know that they're being truly listened to, they share more and feel better, and when they do that they become more capable of doing what they want to do. Two ears, one mouth. Shut up, listen.

But then why would you listen to me?

After all, I'm just a coach.

What They Say

"I loved working with Cleggy during my time at Manchester United. Whatever day you came into the gym, whatever was going on in his life, whatever was going on in your life, whatever had been happening out on the pitch, you could always count on the same thing in Cleggy's gym: he would be unbelievably enthusiastic about what he was doing and nothing from the outside would get in the way. It was very clear that you were in the gym and everything else had to stay outside, which was very refreshing and got the best out of us as footballers.

"Cleggy's a talker. He'd tell you these stories that would have you thinking: *Wow, this guy's away with the fairies*. Other days you'd realise that he was talking total sense. He's got a unique outlook that was different to anything I knew. He had his quirky little ways and he'd get away with saying daft stuff – which not many people could – because he was straight and honest with you and, fundamentally, he was so good at what he did.

"I was sceptical of the role of gym work for a footballer. The majority of players in my generation were brought up to believe that the gym would make you too big to do your job properly. Overdo the weights in there and you'll be too bulky out on the pitch when you need to be really nimble and mobile. In the end, I was at my fittest in my whole life when I was working with Cleggy because he sold it to me.

"We did so much reaction work, hand-eye coordination drills and a lot with bench and bodyweight work, so he was really good for me and he basically changed the way I thought about the gym. I recognise now how hugely important that work was during my career and in retirement, and he was the catalyst for me in that sense.

"His kids are really good weightlifters and that goes a long way to ensure that you trust the person you're working with. Cleggy talked a good game, but he also put out his workload. One of the things that was so great about him was that he did the work with you. You come across some coaches who give you certain workouts to do, and you look at them and you know full-well that they couldn't even do half of what they were asking you to do, but Cleggy did it with you and would then go and do the work with another player after you, and then another player after them. He might be a little fella, but he can do it too."

Rio Ferdinand, Manchester United 2002-2014

"Mick is old school, but an innovator. When you go through injuries and you have problems, you need somebody who can motivate you and Mick was an expert at that. He's a great character full of energy and he's a person you just want to be around."

Louis Saha, Manchester United 2004-2008

"He's a good lad, Mick. I wouldn't expect anything other than the best from him because he's very thorough, very professional and he was really good at United. He had a nice way with him where he was firm but never lost his temper. There was a nice respect for him from all the players and staff, but that only came from him and how he laid the law down in the first place."

Teddy Sheringham, Manchester United 1997-2001

"I liked working with Mick; he had a different approach to others. Being injured a lot, I spent almost two years working out in the gym. To do it for that long, it was great to have somebody there who could inspire you, and also come up with new exercises and different ways of thinking. When you're injured and working out, you need inspiration and people who will take care of you, and working with Mick most definitely helped me at that difficult point in my life."

Jesper Blomqvist, Manchester United 1998-2002

"Mick and I grew very close during my time out with injury. I spent around 15 months injured, and for probably 12 of those I spent every day with him. As a person, he was massive in my return to football and the career I enjoyed. He was inspirational in terms of keeping my motivation up, and his training methods were just as inspiring. We worked well together, bounced off each other and struck up a great relationship.

"When you're going down the road to recovery, sometimes you wonder if there will ever be an end to it, but even though I was in the gym or in the pool, I enjoyed every day just because of Mick's company. He even came to see me in America to do more work in the off-season.

"I think we got on well because we have a similar work ethic. Whoever you are, if you give Mick everything and work hard, he'll love you forever. That's why he and United went so well together. He was an integral part of the club's success during his time there. Just from speaking with other players at United, there's no question that everybody had so much respect for him. He never shouted about the work he did, he just got on with his job, but he was so highly thought of by every player he worked with."

Alan Smith, Manchester United 2004-2007

"Mick and I worked together a lot and he's a good guy. For us he was great to work with. Back then, we were working in the gym and it was totally different to how it is now. When I was over in Manchester and injured my Achilles tendon, I had an operation and spent weeks in the gym and I loved to work with Mick. He's a hard worker. He loves to work hard and to push people and that's what I like too."

Jaap Stam, Manchester United 1998-2001

"I thought Mick was different class. He motivates you. When I was injured, he trained with me every single day and there was never a 'no' in his vocabulary. He'd always encourage me to have a session with him, so I got really close with him throughout the couple of years I was injured. We developed a really, really good relationship as a result. He's a top man."

Ole Gunnar Solskjaer, Manchester United 1996-2007

"Cleggy's a bit quirky, a bit different, he does things his own way, but he would adapt to each situation, each individual and he really cared about you. He wanted you to be a better athlete. He realised the most important thing was out on the pitch, but if he could give that little bit extra with the work that he'd done, then his job would be done.

"You want someone as a coach who can make you that

bit better, whether it be on the pitch or in the gym. What I liked about Cleggy was that he was open-minded and he never wanted to stand still. He was constantly trying different things and I was always like that too; it was just getting that little one or two percent extra to make you a better footballer.

"I think his work did make a difference to my career. Before Cleggy was there, I never really went in the gym, and it went from being a chore to actually being a part of your training, and that was something, along with the yoga that I did, that complemented what I was doing on the pitch. Cleggy knew he was lucky too, because he was working with a dressing room full of players who were open-minded winners who wanted to better themselves.

"Within that, Cleggy was someone who we could relate to and somebody who would help you.

"He was respected by all the players, because he would give you time and ultimately he wanted to make you a better footballer and athlete. He was constantly looking for different ways of doing that."

Ryan Giggs, Manchester United 1990-2014

"I really enjoyed working with Mick. He was certainly different! We had a bit of a power struggle at first, but in the end we conformed and got on really well. Gym work in my day was totally different to what it is now – it was more about upper body work, weights and so on, but Mick had a way of making everything fresh and introducing new things. I loved doing boxing, which was a change for us as footballers, and it was all good. I thoroughly enjoyed working with him, I really did."

Andy Cole, Manchester United 1995-2002

"When you knew you were working with Cleggy, straight away, you're thinking: 'It'll be hard work today,' but the way he went about it meant that you were never dreading it. You always knew that everything he did was going to be of some benefit to you. That was the main thing: there was always a reason behind why you were doing a particular thing. When you see the results of what some lads gained from it and the belief they took from it, it was a major part of their development as footballers. The good thing with Cleggy was that he would give you a bollocking if you needed it, but in a good way. He'd make you understand why. At United at the time with the characters in there and the fierce competition for places, a bit of work with Cleggy could make that little bit of difference to keep you in the team or get you back in the team."

John O'Shea, Manchester United 1999-2011

"I have only positive things to say about Mick. He is who he is; he won't change that for other people, no matter how well-known they are. The way Mick looks at things and sees things is incredible. He's very authentic and that's a great personal ability. He was a fantastic guy and a great professional. He knows what to do with each individual.

"He hasn't got a standard programme which he throws at everybody – he really looks at each person, their bodies and how he can work with that. That really comes off. Also, for me he was really inspirational as well. It wasn't just lifting weights, it was also talking about everything, in life, in the game, in sports in general. He would talk about what makes the best stand out and why, and it was really fantastic to work with him. He is great to talk to, and it was a great partnership between him and Manchester United. He was the fittest guy in the world! I'd go in for a session with him and he'd do it too, then it would be Rio, then Giggsy and others. It was player after player and they weren't easy sessions, but Mick did all of them. He was in his mid-40s and we're all thinking: *Jesus, the level he pushes himself to is amazing*. He was an example for us. He made you want to go to the gym, which is not easy."

Ruud van Nistelrooy, Manchester United 2001-2006

"I had a good few injuries when I was at United and I probably saw Cleggy every day. It's difficult sometimes to be in the mood for gym work, but he's the sort of character to get you in the mood. He's a top man all round, and he wasn't specifically just about lifting weights; he would help you in all the ways you wanted to make gains in certain aspects of your body. He would always take that into consideration. He's an all-round top man.

"I used to enjoy boxing sessions with him in particular. We used to do three lots of 30 seconds and that was it, done. I don't know how you could do any more than that! We did a lot of that, especially in pre-season. It's good for your general fitness, it gets everything going and Cleggy knew the benefits of it. He's pretty fair, Cleggy. There are some people who like the gym and some who don't, but he'd still make you do everything that you had set out to do, and he knew how to encourage you in the way that you needed if you couldn't really be bothered that day. Once you got in there with him, you got everything done."

Wes Brown, Manchester United 1998-2011

"Mick was a joy to work with, someone passionate about his work and his weights. I saw a lot of him and felt that he worked hard to strengthen me. He was professional, friendly and always tried to help – he started boxing with me to sharpen my reactions, even though he was busy and had other players to work with."

Diego Forlan, Manchester United 2002-2004

"Working with Mick was inspirational through his attitude towards life, as well as the energy he brought over to us players to keep us all going at difficult moments in our rehab or daily programmes. To this day, I am still using his abdominal workout in my life after football, although of course not quite in the same numbers! He's a top guy!"

Edwin van der Sar, Manchester United 2005-2011

"I have great memories of working with Mick. Through the use of squat exercises and other forms of training, such as boxing, he helped me make really important improvements to my strength levels."

Patrice Evra, Manchester United 2006-2014

"I found Mick really good to work with, especially during my first three or four years in England, when I had a lot of work to do. I had lots of personal sessions with him and really enjoyed them. His biggest attribute is that he is very positive – he was doing every session with me and he really encouraged me through them. He worked with a lot of individuals and he was a big part of the success we all enjoyed as a team."

Nemanja Vidic, Manchester United 2006-2014

"One way or another, Mick will make an instant impression on you. It doesn't matter who you are, whether you're the best player in the world or the youngest lad coming in as a scholar, he treats everyone the same. When you meet him – especially for me as a young lad having started with him at 15 – you're thinking: *Wow*, but then you see he's the same with the first team and you see that he's treating everyone the same.

"It was his gym; you were under no illusions and he was going to get out of you what he wanted to get out of you in that session. If you didn't, then you could piss off. Mick was ahead of his time. Things that clubs are doing now, he was doing 11 or 12 years before them. Weights in football, nobody did them. Everyone just looked at you like you were mental, but he came in and started lads on press-ups, dips, squatting, chin-ups and all that, but first team players bought into it like Roy Keane. He was one of the first, and as soon as someone like Roy does, everyone follows. Stuff that Mick was doing is now done at every football club around the world.

"We've got a really good relationship. There were times when I worked with Mick every day for three or four months, then I'd go six months without seeing him, but every time you do see him it's exactly the same. It didn't start out rosy; we clashed a little bit, believe it or not. I was the youngest in full time training when I was 15, Mick came in and I'd never been around a football club before. The first time I was injured, I broke my foot and being very, very slightly built, I was a bit embarrassed of doing gym stuff because the weights I would lift were very small. I didn't want people around seeing me doing it, so I would almost shy away from it, which in Mick Clegg's gym just doesn't happen. He actually sat me down one day and had a bit of a go at me, saying I needed to look at my physique if I was going to play in the first team.

"I was listening, but I was still young, and two weeks later we played a hockey match and I'd like to say I ragdolled him around the pitch! Afterwards he came up to me and almost apologised and said: 'I hadn't realised how strong you were, but imagine if you did extra work as well to add to that, how much of an athlete you'd be.' From that moment, we built a relationship up from there.

"When I was coming back from ulcerative colitis, I went to Mick's gym in Ashton for extra sessions because I knew he'd get the best out of me. Sometimes you need extra motivation. I knew that he'd be looking out for my best interests and he'd push me harder than most people would. You like to think you push yourself far, but you've always got more in you. I always respond to a challenge. I know Mick got that extra five, ten percent out of me that helped me come back from the position I was in."

Darren Fletcher, Manchester United 1995-2015

"I was looking for something new after leaving the Great Britain taekwondo setup, and my first session with Mick was so different to anything I'd ever done before. His training methods are completely out of the box, which was great for me. It's so intriguing to hear about who he's worked with, what they're like, how he's trained them, and the fact that he trains everyone differently is what I love about him; he treats everyone as an individual. What I was used to with the GB team was that we'd all have the same weight programme and we never spent the time needed individually, but he knew exactly what I needed to do. We just clicked straight away and that was it. After training with him I became a different athlete, mentally and physically. When I first met Mick, I was 19, ranked seventh in the world. Working with him for just a year got me back to world number one and in amazing shape. He's crazy, but he's so down to earth and what you see is what you get. He'll never let you slack off. He's always on you and he'll give you a hard time, but that's what I needed. I went six competitions – 24 matches – unbeaten, which was my longest run ever. He gets so involved that it feels like there's a part of him in what you're working towards, and that's what's great about him."

Aaron Cook, former Taekwondo world champion

"Mick's very creative with his own unique style. I was a full-time Team GB athlete in taekwondo and Aaron, my boyfriend, was bigging up Mick, telling me about his different styles, about how he was coaching in a way that we hadn't really seen before, so I decided to go with him to do an extra session here and there. I fell in love with it straight away. Once I'd seen what he was doing, I didn't want to miss out on it.

"I think it did help me get to the next level, especially when I was injured. I was able to go somewhere else, add something new to my approach. It allowed me to be more creative, more individual. Mick made me feel like I could do anything, like I was the best in the room, and I think that helped because I then became world champion. I have to thank him for every little part of it.

"I'm still competing but I've also started coaching, and Mick has influenced my approach to that as well. He's shown me that there's no one set way that you have to go. If you truly believe in what you want to do and work hard for it, you can get there. He's shown me that you don't need the fanciest equipment or the biggest gym space, you just need the character and the spirit to do the work no matter where you are. That's what counts more than anything."

Bianca Walkden, taekwondo world champion

"Mick is a highly intelligent individual and a creative genius in terms of innovating to bring the best out of athletes. He is always looking for new ways to work and that is refreshing for athletes – they never have time to be bored. In taekwondo you require explosion, power, endurance, speed and other physical attributes, but intelligence is also key and Mick has shown he is able to improve the cognitive ability of my students. If you take the example of Aaron Cook working with Mick, he went through a run where he took medals from nine of ten events, and he was injured in the one where he didn't. That's incredible. I went from having an athlete on my hands to having a super athlete."

Patrice Remarck, former taekwondo coach of Aaron Cook

"I started working with Mick in 2018 when we were introduced by another speedway rider, Kyle Howarth. There's only so far that you can go with training and going to the gym yourself, so when I wanted somebody who could take me to the next level, Mick was the only option for me. I needed something different to further my career, and his work with brain training and reactions had a massive impact on me.

"It's very old school in his lab: no mirrors, no music, no dicking about or you'll be out of that door before you know it. He gave me all the personal attention and level of detail that I needed to become British champion within a year of starting work with him, and I can honestly say that I wouldn't be where I am today without his help. He was absolutely brilliant in terms of developing my mindset and showing me how to be the best. Mick just sees what's in you and, beyond that, what potential is in you. He's worked with the best of the best in football, but he knew exactly what needed to be done to succeed in speedway, which is about as far removed from football as you can imagine. He just understands what each athlete needs."

Charles Wright, British Speedway champion

"I feel I like had the best childhood ever. Growing up in and around Olympic Sports Gym provided an anchor for everything I knew and gave me a unique start in life. I was forever being challenged by my dad, which I loved. He paid for me to have Maths and English tutors at primary school because of the importance of good grades. Typically, he even went above and beyond when it came to picking the influences around me. One tutor, Dave Sanderson, didn't just teach maths; he was also a national triple jumper and we ended up training together after lessons. Those experiences were invaluable to me, both academically and athletically.

"Dad delivered very clear communication which taught me some very healthy lessons – too many to list here – but one that I'll always remember is that first impressions last. When I was a promising footballer in my early teens, I couldn't quite understand why I hadn't been scouted by a professional club. Dad said he had a theory which could help. I demanded to know what it was. So, he fetched a football and told me to stand by it in a power position. Next thing I know, the ball is miles away and I'm up in the air. He said: 'If you tackle like that, with your playing ability, I think you could make it.' I harnessed that feeling and that information, took them into my game and, despite being quite small, I was soon really limiting my opponents' ability to impact on the game. Within long I'd been scouted by Manchester United and I began living the dream of being a professional footballer.

"Lessons like that were a masterstroke by my dad, who always wanted the best for all his children. He worked hard, he studied and he had a way about him that you just knew he was capable of anything. Whatever he was involved in, he gave it one hundred percent to become the best version of himself and help others to do the same. I'm deeply proud to have followed in his coaching footsteps after my football career finished, and I'm proud to pass on the beliefs, principles and wisdom he handed down to me and my siblings. Through the bloodline, down the years, I hope my children, their children and beyond will always have the same spirit and creativity that began with my dad. If they have, then anything they want is possible."

Michael Clegg

"Being the youngest of five siblings teaches you a lot about hierarchy, especially when you're the youngest by seven years, but my siblings played a huge part in my life. When I was around six, I noticed that they were always bringing home trophies and sporting these huge grins like they'd just discovered how to save the world. Football, weightlifting, basketball, swimming… every week it seemed to be something new but, despite their happiness, nobody ever went on about how good they were.

"Everybody was successful but humble and I suppose, being in that kind of environment, it was inevitable that I'd follow them down the same kind of path. I became a weightlifter and, over the course of 12 years, I ended up competing around the world; not something that could be seen as a realistic ambition for a lad from Ashton-under-Lyne, but then that stemmed from the upbringing I had, where nothing was unrealistic and anything was possible if you put the work in.

"All along the way, I was coached by my dad not just to weightlift, but also to become a coach, and that's what I've been doing since I hung up my weightlifting boots in 2016. Working with him is a test, and I mean that in a positive way. You'll very rarely get full instructions or direction in what you should be doing – he likes to put pressure on people and see what they come up with once they've interpreted what he wants. He calls it chaos training and it gets results. Under test conditions, under pressure, you learn a lot about yourself, and much of what I've learned about myself in life stems from the time I've spent with my dad."

Shaun Clegg

"I am really proud to run Olympic Sports Gym with my two brothers, Steven and Mark. Family-run gyms are very much a thing of the past with the rise of commercial gyms, plus many independent gyms that have a similar demographic to ours have a dark undertone of money-laundering or selling steroids to supplement potential earnings. My dad has always been strongly against anything of this nature, which I believe has been internalised by myself and my brothers. By not succumbing to any shortcuts to earn money we have a real family-friendly, inclusive gym.

"Ashton-under-Lyne is in one of the deprived wards in England, and I think it is important in places like this that people and young people have a place to blow off steam and are able to feel part of a community. We make a point of buying flags from all the different countries that our members come from, just to try and make them feel included, and this has created an accepting, multicultural culture within our gym. We allow parents to bring children to train them from the age of 11 as we strongly believe that early exposure to training can provide an escapism from some of the pressure our young people face.

"My daughter, Katie, really got into her training in her early teenage years and it has helped to shape her into the disciplined, ambitious and successful young woman she is now. At 13, she was on the cusp of exclusion from mainstream education. Six years on, she is studying Law at the University of Manchester. I can see that sport, in some way, saved her. Growing up with our dad, we all went to the gym from a young age, we know its benefits and we want to pass this on."

Mandy Clegg

"As a young kid, I had no sporting interest whatsoever. As I reached the age of 12, I wouldn't get involved in any kind of sport and I would actually forget my PE kit on purpose so that I didn't have to partake. By the time I turned 14, after working with my dad, I was clean-and-jerking 100kg and part of the Great Britain Schoolboy weightlifting squad. Over the years that followed, I went around Europe representing Great Britain in junior events and notched over 30 national records in various age groups before becoming the British senior champion at 19. Alongside this, I was part of our school basketball team which twice entered the English Schools Championships (exiting to Wes Brown's Burnage High School in the semi-finals of the Northern division both times), I represented the school at shot put and volleyball, so it's fair to say that the training I did with my dad had a profound impact on how things panned out for me."

Mark Clegg

"You're a creature of your environment, as they say, so because we grew up in a gym environment, everything's been about training, all my life and all of my siblings' lives. I think I was three years old when my dad had me tidying up the 1.5kg and 2.5kg discs in Olympic! Dad took us everywhere and went out of his way to make sure he took us to practice. He liked the idea of us doing lots of sports, so he took us everywhere from a young age and gave us the best opportunities to excel. We were always training at the gym or watching sports.

"I remember watching the Rocky movies, and Rocky's trainer, Mickey, reminds me of my dad in some ways. Dad has those same old school methods. His approach is underpinned by science and technology, but fundamentally it's about passion, which rubs off on his clients.

"He likes to shout now and again, but that's because he wants you to succeed and it replicates the pressure of high-level sport. He really knows how to get into your head and get the best out of you. I think that's why he got on with Roy Keane and Sir Alex Ferguson so well – it's all about winning and coming first. He's a born winner. Even now, he's knocking on a bit but he keeps himself very fit and really looks after himself.

"I love running Olympic with Mark and Mandy – the gym's

been open almost 40 years and I hope we keep on going for at least another 40 years. I want to have my kids tidying up the 1.5kg and 2.5kg discs, like we were with my dad."

Steven Clegg